~Renunciation ~

~Implementing the dharma for release from addiction~

Jonathan M. King.

Edition -1-2015

ISBN:10:1511809965
ISBN:13:9781511809962

May the teachings herein help you as they

have helped me,

This book is dedicated to you!

How to use this book

Do not read the end first.

Carry out the daily meditations!

Every day!!

Read the amount you require for you meditations then stop.

(I recommend one chapter per sitting).

At the end of each chapter is a blank page for notes.

Follow each step if it is not understood re-read it unless otherwise instructed.

Do not try to read this in one sitting.

The ten chapters represent the ten steps to release from suffering.

CONTENTS

A Note from the Author

I remember the day I discovered that I really had quit. It was by accident. I used to quit regularly using the Allen Carr technique- *Easy way to control alcohol* which I highly recommend. The only problem with it was it was always a temporary fix. I would read it and stop for good. Within 3 to 6 months I would have started again. It had become so normal to do this that I would use it and *expect* to start again, I was just so grateful for the short lived but much needed break.

It was during such a period of abstinence in which I started reading the *Tibetan Book of Living and Dying*. I had started meditating thanks to this wonderful book and was about 6 months sober at the time. I loved it and started noticing rapid changes in the way I responded to the world. I dove deeply into the philosophy of (Tibetan) Buddhism reading anything I could get my hands on and took to it like a fish to water. I was sleeping better, my stress levels were down, my ability to concentrate had drastically improved. It seemed as though I had found peace with the world. This was about to be put to the test!

A few months later I was at a party and, well it was time, so I started drinking again, just to be sociable you understand. After about two weeks of not enjoying it, I noticed my intake increasing as usual. It had started to effect my mind which had become so sharp and at the same time peacefull through meditation. This was annoying. I realized that I was unable to find my *chi-spot!* It was obvious to me that I would not be able to do both, something would have to go. It was no contest. I was being offered a choice between slipping back into the miserable dull horror I had always known or a new road adorned with all the trappings of "Nirvana". In a flash I could see, it wasn't even a question of making up my mind. I had looked just beyond the dualistic nature of my predicament and glimpsed into a space where there *was no do or don't.* All of the stuff was still there, the reasons I abused myself, the consequences of my actions, I could see the old desires hanging in the air, I simply no longer had an opinion about them. At that moment I knew I had *already* quit forever, before the question was asked and without pain or suffering.

A simple choice had presented itself at the right time, in the right place and made me an offer. Strangely enough reverting to my old habits and once again being confronted by the choice, *but with the new understanding that I would lose my new way of being,* alerted me to the fact that my perspective had changed. Sure, I could continue and escalate my intake until I was back to square one but that road was merely old habit. The understanding was that I had had enough pain and suffering, the shadow that had been with me my whole life was *already* gone. As gone as when Frodo threw the ring into the fires of mount Doom, vanished as if it never was. I had stumbled, completely by accident, upon the understanding of dropping attachments and addictions. This is a moment of enlightenment, as is described in Buddhist teachings regarding recognition of attachment to external objects to create false happiness and identity. If these teachings are truly understood and carefully implemented, modern world attachments,

they-simply-fade-away!

Since then I have honed the technique, delved still deeper into my studies and gone beyond certain thresh holds in relation to understanding the true nature of attachments. I have become a student of Dzogchen Buddhism, an apprentice Bodhisattva, and as a such, it is my duty to share it. This project is the result. A modern technique using ancient philosophy to just let go of what is not at home in our make up. Quick and painless. I wish you luck with eliminating your attachments....

Although I know you don't need it!

*

Introduction

Meditation will increase your ability to concentrate, sleep (if you can't sleep), relax, deal with stress and conflict, stop addictions and improve (or terminate) relationships. It will quickly enhance your general quality of life whilst helping to discover or re-connect with your purpose in life. Meditation will also create a balance between the highs and lows of life, such as feelings of euphoria expirienced when enjoying hobbies as opposed to the downer of going to work when you don't feel like it. These are all achieved through training of the mind during meditation. When practiced correctly, *Rigpa* is achieved; the natural state of mind (more about that later).

And mindfulness? Mindfulness is a particular method of focusing attention on the present moment while utilizing all the available faculties of the mind. The objective? To help us utilize and place our attention where and in a way that it can be most beneficial. Mindfulness is a method of honing the sharpness of the mind, improving its ability to annalise and contemplate whilst not being bound by external junk. Meditation will bring us to a space of calm and stillness and it is from this space that we can most effectively apply mindfulness to steer the mind efficiently.

The goal of mindfulness is to achieve something called *Special Insight*. This involves gaining insight into the true nature of the object upon which you have placed your attention. Sounds weird? Imagine if everything you turned your attention towards had a different reality than that which you percieve it to be, even your addiction...Ultimately this encompasses an understanding of emptiness, unity and selflessness.

(Keep an open mind, all will be revealed in time).

The Dalai Lama states that humanity has one common denominator in which we are able to recognize our oneness or common unity;

Every human wants to avoid suffering and has a desire to seek happiness.

Meditation is the beginning of you achieving these things. Suffering is humanities alarm bell. It will chime when we are responding to negative karma. Karma is a very real thing, it can be measured and it's active all day long in everything we do. It is an integral part of our struggle for happiness, and all of our suffering. Buddhism explains it as a re-occurring lesson which is the result of past actions in this life or the previous one. The point being, if we have acted in a negative manner, going against the grain of a sort of universal morality and this has had a knock on effect on people, enemies, friends, animals or the planet, then we have created an anomaly. Karma of course is not only negative, and creating positive karma (positive traveling energy) is our primary directive as human beings.

When negative, afflictive emotions are at work, or karma creates mischief occurring with regularity and tending to outweigh positive karma, then one of three things happen;

- A revolution; or reaction which will drive the individual to fight against his personal directives.

- Normalcy bias; An adjustment of social boundaries is put in place to create room for unacceptable behavior, making it tolerated behavior and thus blending it into the new status quo.

- War; in which an individual is in turmoil with himself and knows it but must continue to support both elements of his dilemma. This is called schizophrenia.

The theory behind karma is that we are trapped in a cyclic existence (Samsara) in which the same set of circumstances brings us the same set of situations until we decide that we are doing something wrong. Eventually we are forced to observe the motivation for the action. If we are truly honest with ourselves, do we not come to the inescapable conclusion that our perception of reality, our perspective is causing the problem.

Why must this be cyclical?

Good question, you would think if we were smart we would simply say

"Oh that's no good we had better scrap that idea and start again".

Allas we don't because of deep seated programming creating a blind spot and the fact that we are slow un-learners. It's all around us and all too often we take the result of our negative emotions and bad programming to be -the way things go. We do it individually but we also do it collectively, and just like sheep or lemmings we think

"It must be o.k., everybody else does it."

A recent example of this on a collective level would be the 2008 bank bailouts which did nothing to fix the financial problem or curb the practices which brought it to us in the first place! We simply exacerbated and perpetuated the situation. Perhaps when we do start to react to our negative karma in an effective manner, the Samsaric nature of our reality will also evolve. That truly would herald a paradigm shift!

The greatest problem we have to face, as humans and victims of drug abuse, is realizing that our redundant system which can only be sustained in a world of infinite resources, stimulates us to respond to our outside world in exactly the *wrong way to thrive!* Our way of surviving as a species has invaded and rewired our individual psyche. This seeps right down from the boardroom behavior of corporations, bankers and politicians into the infant rooms of mothers and fathers teaching their children what is best for them, what to like and what to dislike, who to love and who to hate or fear, how to succeed...

Without co-operation in nature karma would not exist and neither would we. The misperception that we must fence ourselves off from our fellows creates the disharmony. We are a well organized society but our co-operation is held in check by the understanding that our actions have consequences within our financial, social and legal systems. This system of control creates a forced co-operation insinuating oppression and this does not build a perspective of empathy and compassion. Beneath the hum of modern life is a deep under current of discontentment and primordial aggression.

What does this have to do with me and my hang over you ask?

This misperception creates crazy people. Unfortunately that's just about everybody here inclusive of your good self! The real misperception is;

that first world man chose not to look further than the end of his own nose in the hunt for gratification and such gratification is short lived!

We are behaving as if the worlds resources are infinite, but deep down we know this is not so. Scarcity is all around, this is how the economy works. We have become so estranged from what living is all about that we don't even really consider it anymore. Things of true value have become replaced by trinkets and tricks which hold absolutely no intrinsic value what so ever. Money itself has been worthless since it was uncoupled from the gold standard in the 70's and attached to the wall street standard, and yet it has become more important than ever! I am not suggesting that we didn't have drug addicts before the 70's of course, I am stating that our madness and our perspective of reality becomes more detached from truth with each passing decade. It has everything to do with our hangovers and or the reason we can't pick up the phone without a cigarette!

Our recognition of true value is distorted and we are ever becoming more estranged from reality!

The only way to break this habit is to alter our perception to encompass a broader view, and this is where meditation steps in. Herman Hesse wrote the following:

There is no reality except the one contained within us.

Take a minute to think about that. It means simply this, *The choice is yours.* The pathway laid out hierin offers us a steadfast ability to recognize and listen to our inner truth or inner voice if you like. It is quiet but it is always there. Through meditation we can change our lives so that even in a world such as the one we have built, we may see the deeper truth and beauty of this life. Brain washing takes time to reverse and this is literally what is required, the reversal of brain washing. False truths about the world we live in are the reasons behind our anger, frustration, lust, jealousy, depression, addiction, poverty and the list goes on. This pathway will give you the power to manifest your life as you wish.

Where attention goes, energy flows, and where energy flows, things grow.

An old Indian sat his grand son down to tell him a story

"Son, in every man there live two wolves,

One is full of wisdom, peace, courage and love, and the other, full of hate, animosity, jealousy and anger.

They are at war with

one another and will fight constantly."

He paused while the young boy thought for a moment.

The boy asked

"Which one wins Grandpa"?

The old man answered

"The one you feed."

*

Chapter 1

The Right Start

In taking on this book, path, way, project, you will become what is called a apprentice Bodhisattva. This means that you will discover another way of being that is much more satisfactory to the one you are presently in. It doesn't mean that you will join a sect, move to India and give all your money to the Bhagwan. What is a Bodhisattva? The first thing that pops up when I Google it is this;

The term "Bodhisattva" was used by the Buddha to refer to himself both in his previous lives and as a young man in his current life, prior to his enlightenment, in the period during which he was working towards his own liberation. When, during his discourses, he recounts his experiences as a young aspirant, he regularly uses the phrase "When I was an unenlightened bodhisattva..." The term therefore connotes a being who is "bound for enlightenment", in other words, a person whose aim is to become fully enlightened. The bodhisattva is also described as someone who is still subject to birth, illness, death, sorrow, defilement, and delusion.

~Definition borrowed from wikipedia.~

It's just a word, but in following the teachings of this book/ course or whatever you want to call it, we happen to utilize meditation and teachings which are borrowed from Tibetan Buddhism (Dzogchen) and so for the sake of argument I use their lingo. It does mean that you are going to take a vow. Just as a Bodhisattva takes a vow of life long compassion towards his fellow man and a monastic life of altruism, you are going to take a vow to control your attachment for the good of yourself and those you care about. This is going to be a life long commitment and while I know that statement sparks fear in the heart of any person who has fallen into the trap of holding wrong views regarding substance abuse, I also know that this can be achieved by anyone who has an I.Q. which allows them to tie their own shoe laces. Plus once you have taken this leap you will feel elated and,

you will not miss anything from your old way of being.

Quitting with the right method is painless and can even be enjoyable. It doesn't mean getting involved in a religion as you would if you were to go to AA meetings. Buddhism is also a philosophy and the teachings, as in many religions, discuss the relationship between the everyday man and his *attachment* to worldly possessions as opposed to the deeper man and his connection with something called *"Ultimate Truth"*. Here is the Buddhist explanation of that term which will make no sense at all;

The Buddhist doctrine of **the two truths** *differentiates between two levels of truth in Buddhist discourse: relative or commonsensical truth, and absolute or ultimate truth. In Tibetan Buddhism ultimate truth is synonymous with emptiness.*

They're big on emptiness, never mind all will be revealed in time. For the time being when the term emptiness pops up think of it as unity among living beings, life itself being our basic common denominator. So, as of now you are an apprentice Bodhisattva about to set off on an adventure in search of ultimate truth in the hope that you can quickly and easily deal with your problem.

You have come to the right place!

Congratulations, and I mean it sincerely. It means you have been through hell and have found yourself here. Here is where it stops. I am the proof and like me, this book is for you if you know you have a problem and you know you need help to stop. It is not for the person who isn't sure and maybe would like to do it less...bla bla bla. If you are serious and can fully comprehend the steps herein, this will work for you. The wonderful side effect to this method is that you gain an understanding of some beautiful techniques and insights which offer tools for life that you will carry with you to the end of your days. Without your addictions that may be a long time.

I would like to offer my excuses in advance, this first chapter can be confronting but it is necessary, so for those who take offence, try to bite the bullet. An open mind is crucial to success! Think of this book as a jigsaw puzzle, if you miss a piece you will never see the whole picture, so it's important to *make sure that the essence of each chapter is understood before moving on to the next,* then you will not fail. Speaking of which, that was **the first instruction.**

What is meant by <u>proper contemplation</u>? It is properly establishing the definitive and interpretable sutras. When Bodhisattva's are free of doubt, they can meditate single pointedly. Otherwise, if doubt and indecision beset them, *they will be like a man at a cross roads uncertain which path to follow.*

This means simply to <u>understand the teachings fully,</u> or to take the time to immerse your self in each chapter while maintaining an open mind. In any case, once you have done so the text suggests you go forth with out doubt and with;

a firm conviction that you are following the right path

There is no dead line here so time is o.k. You don't necessarily have to change anything whilst using this program but you do need to invest *regular* practice time and be *consistent with the study.* This is important, so if you take 3 weeks or 3 months it is of no consequence.

In this chapter I would like to discuss the the relationship between us humans and our addictions which will from now on fall under the category of *attachments*. Addiction is a foul word which implies that the person under the influence or evil persuasion of a substance because they are weak willed or that they are some sort of criminal or member of the dark underbelly of society. Let's make it clear right now that a person who is behaving as a so-called drug addict or smoker is merely someone who is unfortunate enough to have fallen prey to a scam which revolves around human habit forming.

Habit; routine patterns of behavior that are repeated regularly and that tend to occur subconsciously.

As for criminal behavior, the government makes enough money taxing the sale of the biggest death drugs on the planet. They condone them and (until recently) allow corporations to advertise blatantly. In fact they would allow it tomorrow if they weren't scared of losing votes. I would suggest that politicians and corporate profiteers are a much better representation of the the the dirty underbelly of society rather than anyone who simply fell for their crap. Any way, regarding your habit, that is the way it will be thought of from now on, nothing more than going to the toilet or responding to an itch. Habitual negative behavior does however present some nasty side effects which is why you are here. Admitting that one has a problem can be scary but there are always two sides to every coin. On the one hand you have realized that you need help to quit which often causes panic and fear to step in

"Oh no, I am attached"!!

On the other hand all you are admitting is that the object of your attachment, beit drink, cigarettes, negative sexuality, cocaine, work, dysfunctionality within a relationship, all of the above, are things that you have allowed to slip into a space in which they have become *routine patterns* of behavior that are repeated regularly and that tend to occur *subconsciously*. And that is no big deal, there is a simple cure, my message at this point is to relax. Sweat, have the headache, feel nauseas, have a cigarette if you want but relax and ease on into the cure. I know that if you are in the grip of "the fear" (psychosis created by recent abuse) that me saying "it's no big deal" will seem to you as though I have no idea what I am talking about but I am telling you the truth. What ever horror you may be stuck in, it is temporary and the permanent cure is quick and painless. At least after you have finished the book it's quick and painless. Oh yeah you don't have to quit or ease up until the books done by which time you will be *craving to quit!* I promise. And unlike other techniques, you will have gained great insight and have a key to carry with you always. That means quit forever without withdrawal problems or renewed desire for the object of your attachment.

Any wounds which may have been opened will heal and any friendships that have been tested can wait until you are in shape to deal with the consequences. True friendship can handle a few knocks. If this has occurred and it *does* require your immediate attention then deal with it, explain your situation and let it go. Explaining to someone that it was the drink/ drug talking and not you and that you are about to do something about it can be helpful regarding patching up a friendship but it can also act as a milestone for you. What's more, letting go of things over which you no longer have control is something you are going to have to get used to. It can be a liberating experience. We are going to look at attachments, recognition of them and meditation designed to put these things in perspective.

A Rant About Attachments

The Birth of Negative Attachment

Humanity is afflicted with a heart breaking struggle for happiness while running head long towards a self imposed suffering.

The above is a rough translation for the Tibetan word Samsara.

Samsara comes about through the illusion that one can find happiness in the world of form. Its root lies in the idea that man is above nature and spirituality. All the big bright colours of the world of form appear to be much more vivid, the noises louder, much more impressive than what one might presume to visualize as;

" a world of inner peace".

Most people cannot even sit still for half an hour let alone meditate, and who would want to, who has the time?

Since birth we are encouraged to chase after elements of this world of form, whether it be to get an ice cream as a child or to get a Porsche later in life. We believe that happiness comes through the title we gain, through becoming the top dog at work, or receiving our PhD, perhaps even getting a spouse with breast implants. This is all food for a false sense of self, and that self will always be hungry. It is this forever grasping and clinging of desire, to have, to become or even to get rid of which causes the paradox of Samsara. This self is the one humanity, more so modern western society, has come to take as The Self, and we defend him to the death....

This is the psychosis which leads to all the worlds suffering.

~Aquarius Agenda-Jonathan M King~

Advertising and television are great examples of attachment-delivery tools. It's a shame our culture reflects teen idols and consumerism as a distraction to our daily lives instead of the reality of the devastating standard of living of 80% of the worlds population. Instead of making right choices based on truth, we find ourselves trying to imitate some expensively dressed, pumped up, nipped and tucked super model which is never going to work hence more internal disharmony and dissatisfaction with what we consider to be the self. It's really quite funny if you think about it: This illusive self is not real and it spends all of its time trying to copy someone else who is unreal! This may not be you but it is an example of our subliminal daily digest. Through T.V. and advertising, we learn consumerism (self gratification) as opposed to compassion (love). The structure of our society demands that we consume (to keep the financial ball rolling) and that we live in fear (so that we don't change the status quo). Why else would so many of us spend our lives going to jobs that we dislike day in day out? Sure some of us love our jobs, I am quite happy with my work but this is not a good example of a general cross section of modern society.

Self gratification and fear are not good bedfellows and it is from this soil that our attachments are grown. It is no wonder that we tend to turn the mind off and look towards escapism for some form of release.

Our biology starts giving us lessons before birth. In the womb we already learn defensive tactics regarding the world outside through the chemical make up of our DNA and this goes on all the way through our lives. Our directive is to constantly try to adapt due to the signals being received from the environment. If we presume our environment, our neighborhood is telling us we need to gather more stuff like a new car, laptop, high pressure water spout to clean the mold off the driveway, then we will blindly follow this instruction but it won't necessarily bring happiness. O.k, maybe for a week but then we are off in search of the next article to consume or hang on the wall. We have replaced what our *biology* is telling us with what our *mind* is telling us.

Due to the impossibility of satisfying this itch we have created a way of living a life revolving around false values, we reach for an affair, the bottle, a fag, something sweet you name it. Any-thing to distract us or sweeten our reality because god knows life is better when you have these things, advertising says so. And hey, every body around us is doin it, it simply must be so, safety in numbers and all! We are like a herd of wildebeest trying to get across a river full of crocodiles. We understand that a few of us will be eaten but 99% will get across. I have news for you, the wildebeest have much better odds than we do! We behave more like lemmings! What's more the wildebeest understand that a few will be eaten, the reasoning being the suffering of a few outweighs the needs of the many in a life and death situation. Our actions are simply insane!

The first requirement for personal growth is the strong desire for change. The second is time, energy and dedication. The reason we don't change easily is because as humans we tend to stick to what we know, definitely if the masses and our peers do it. Moving outside the comfort zone creates cognitive dissonance.

Another reason is that we have faith in our mothers, fathers and teachers. Learned behaviors are most often placed their by people we absolutely trust who have a strong bond with us. Anyone suggesting that our personal beliefs or behavior may be at fault is often the same as them telling our mother off. We don't change until we realize, through repetitive negative feedback from our environment, that something has got to give! This will manifest in one of two ways,

1/ -   *We become repulsed by our present situation.*

2/ -   *A situation from the environment has caused shock or trauma.*

Now we are presented with a choice.

Identification with Attachments

Attachment is nothing more than *association*. Release is then by definition merely breaking ties of *identification*. Since our common human goal is the pursuit of happiness, negative attachment is de- constructive to that process. If you are sending negative signals into your environment you will generally get negativity back in return, the universe is great like that!

Identification with our drug of choice is a habit in which we spend most of our "relaxing time" and it absorbs all of our attention while we are doing it. It has become part of our repertoire. While identifying, we cannot be objective about the object of our identification and we lose control over our own being. Our thoughts and actions are no longer our own. The more we associate the more familiar we become. This familiarity is a form of representation, people also attach you to the object;

"Oh yeah Pete you'll always find him down at the local ready for a pint and a game of snooker".

If we search out the reasons for **association,** we come to perspective. This is what put us in the local with a pint in our hand, our perspective. Our perspective which is born out of the quagmire of fear and self gratification. We could disagree and say

"No I just need to relax".

I would have to ask What from, your loving wife? You married her! Stress? You determine the amount of stressful situations in your life, don't you? I know I do. Or is it that we have become so accustomed to "stress from work", or deluded through our desire to win, get more, be more that we believe relaxing *is* the mind fuck achieved through escapism? Do we believe that life is supposed to be like this? Perhaps you aren't ready to blame society for everything just yet, maybe we just think we started as kids and just got hooked, it was all just peer group pressure. My answer would be what sort of society produces such young peers, and why on earth would such peers place any value on a bottle of poisonous chemicals and rotting vegetable matter? Do not fall into the trap of taking your motivation or perspective on this subject too lightly, that's why you are here in the first place.

Our societies fundamental problem is not even the self centered attitude, that is simply a by product, the real culprit is a **lack of equality**. The minute we start looking over the fence to see what sort of car the neighbor is driving, we are acting out the game. The sister of identification is **comparison** which is also as you may have guessed, a byproduct of the lack of equality among our fellow human beings. Comparison is about judgment, one up man-ship, gossip, jealousy and all the other nasty negative emotions and actions which go with it. It will lead to constant worrying about the self image and what others are thinking about it, the clothes, the look, watching out for what is said, suspicion, paranoia.

These are all little games played out by the I-dentity, while a person in control of his consciousness admires traits in another, the False Self covets them. Similarly while a person in consciousness will notice defective behavior due to unconsciousness in a person, the false self will start judging in order to make himself correct and or better than the other. He also starts looking around for someone to share the news with. Chronic complexes arise in the unconscious person who is constantly absorbed with identification and comparison. This is almost everybody. Schizophrenia, superiority, inferiority, class and race distinction you name it.

Remove the lack of equality within society and you remove the illusion of complex.

This is the house of cards on which the foundation of *your* attachments is built, what ever they may be. The single most important thing to understand right now is this;

It is not your fault

For now try to recognize where your attachment is coming from and to own your part in it as an innocent bystander who's eye's are opening. I know when I look at my roots I find an alcoholic family full of fear and harboring separation issues, all of who would do anything not to be present. Not one of them has been able to maintain a long term loving relationship. The same fear goes as far back as I have been able to dig. I have my recent family history on my mothers side first hand from my grandmother who is 96 at present. Her parents were no exception to the rule. Some of my ancestors have gone to their death under the influence of alcohol or drugs, at least one used it directly to kill herself, all died as users and *all* who have died have done so carrying the scars of their attachments.

You have the chance to live and die in peace and without scars. The biggest killer on this planet is substance abuse which is closely followed by fast foods. Terrorist victims are somewhere down there below death by peanut allergies. See what I mean about our societies program of fear indoctrination and separation?

Some tips and pointers beforehand.

Training the mind is a process of familiarization. The objective of meditation is to **remove defective qualities and improve upon positive qualities.**

Identify the object to be meditated upon whether it is an object or an image of one in your mind. Analyze it then meditate upon it. At this point if I say meditate, I mean try to relax and quieten the mind. The further you read the more in touch you will become with relaxing into meditation. The best way I can explain this in a few words is: Follow your breath and when you find the space between breaths focus on it. This is the feeling of void we are looking for as a starting place. Another concept is to try to find a space in which you are at peace and are not pulling at any idea's (likes) nor pushing away any thoughts, idea's or beliefs (dislikes). These two concepts are abstract and that's o.k., you have to use your imagination. Once you used it to convince yourself that your first cigarette tasted great so I am sure it will work for this. **Motivation** is key to results in meditation.

Why do I meditate?; Through transforming my mind I wish to re-educate myself thus making life more favorable.

This will bring you to a fresh **perspective**, and that's what we want to cultivate.

While notable transformation will occur when we start training, subtle transformation is already occurring. The seed has been planted as we start to eliminate or even simply observe what is wrong and start to assemble favorable conditions for the mind-work. We are going to educate ourselves to automatically search for conducive factors that give rise to happiness because that is, simply put: good for us. It is natural for us to want this and unnatural for us to seek things that are good for us in poison. It just ain't in there. During the process we will be able to abandon the factors that make us miserable. It is much easier to teach some one to take something that is good for them and pleasurable than to teach someone to learn to associate regularly with things that are bad for them and not pleasurable. Your dysfunctional habit is nothing more than a reflex re-action to stimulus which needs replacing.

At this point I feel the need to add a section from the Tibetan Book of Living and Dying to help explain meditation. Sogyal Rinpoche explains with beautiful simplicity;

If your mind is able to settle naturally of its own accord, and if you feel you are inspired simply to rest in its pure awareness, then you do not need any method of meditation. In fact, it might even be unskillful when you're in such a state to try and employ one. However a vast majority of us find it difficult to arrive at this state straight away. We simply do not know how to awaken it, and our minds are so wild and so distracted that we need a skillful means, a method to evoke it. By "skillful" I mean that you bring together your understanding of the essential nature of our mind, your knowledge of your own various shifting moods, and the insight you have developed through your practice into how to work with yourself, from moment to moment. By bringing these together, you learn the art of applying whatever method is appropriate for any particular situation or problem, to transform the environment of your mind.

~Tibetan Book of Living and Dying- Sogyal Rinpoche~

*

I have placed a meditation or as Sogyal Rinpoche says "a skillful means" here to get started (Candle meditation). Our goal for this meditation is for it to act as a doorway to a space of emptiness and stillness so use this as your <u>daily entry point</u>. Eventually new meditations and teachings will be implemented into this nothingness arena which you will find after the candle meditation. But first I suggest you find a quiet place to regularly exercise. It should be a place which you can leave ready for meditation so that minimal effort must be taken to prepare. Ideally a room or space that is not entered or used for other things if possible. It should be a quiet space but again if this is not available find the quietest possible area. Most practitioners will suggest that you sit on the floor in lotus position, look slightly downward, leave the eye's open and stare at the floor just over the end of your nose whilst placing the tongue on the roof of the mouth. All this whilst maintaining a rigidly straight back. Bla, bla, bla...

I don't do this. I don't bend that well anymore! I use a comfortable chair in which I can sit without my elbows getting tangled in arm rests. My palms are folded one on top of the other with thumb points meeting (that last part is traditional). I place a statue of the *Buddha on a small table in front of me with a stomp candle in front of it. The Buddha is about 4 feet in front of me. The statue should be at the same height or higher than your line of vision.

*Any object will do. I use the Buddha but the candle alone will suffice. The flame is a concentration or focal point with which to begin. Meditation for me is a reinforcing of all the qualities represented in the form of the Buddha and this is why I use the statue. Symbolism is an important part of manifesting the idea's of the formless world into the physical world although you should not use guided meditation tapes or music. This is known as *"listening to music"* and has nothing to do with disciplining the mind.

Meditation should be carried out twice each day for 20 minutes minimum per meditation. Morning meditation is the most important as it will set the tune for your day. Periods will extend by themselves when it is time. This will not seem time consuming but necessary and welcome. I recall when I started, twenty minutes seemed like an age, now 1 hour minimum is required in the morning only and it is the best time of the day. Allow this to happen by itself. It may take six weeks it may take six years so do not to get hung up on time. For the purposes of this book you will need only twenty minutes, extend if and when you wish. When you are ready to start this meditation and have relaxed enough to focus, close your eyes and commence.

If you have trouble focusing your concentration in this the first meditation exercise, try the following; When you come to the first doorway, hold the door knob in your hand, feel it. Concentrate on its feel in your hand and look down the length of your arm. Be there. Feel the weight of the door as you pull it shut, hear the click and feel the slight resistance from the door as you pull its weight into the lock. Notice the lessening of the noise of the outside world and the slight darkening of the room before you move on to the next doorway. Visualizing utilizing aspects and preoperties of the five senses within the meditation is a helpful technique to bring yourself into the moment. The false, or grosser self, gets its sense of "I am and that is" through the same five senses so visualizing them in action is a good technique to help build bridges from the world of form to the formless or to the more subtle levels of self.

Basic Tool-Starters Meditation

-Candle Meditation-

Imagine you are in a room, it is dark outside and slightly stormy. There is a candle on the table which is affected by the draft running through the house. This central room is the arena of your mind, the candle is your minds focus and the winds testing the flame are representative of your thoughts whistling in from the outside world.

There are 10 doorways to this room. You are about to count to 10 and with each count you will breathe out and as you exhale you release thoughts. In the space between breathing out and in there is a space. This is a space of emptiness and stillness. While focusing on this emptiness you shut one of the entrances to the room and as you breathe in you walk to the next exit. As you shut these doorways to the outside world one by one, the room becomes darker and quieter, your thoughts become still. With each closing entryway the flame becomes more resilient in the center of the room. When you have exhaled and arrived at 10, the last draft entrance is closed, darkness outside the circumference of light created by the now steady, unflinching candle flame is complete. The mind is also still, as one by one, the thoughts of your everyday man or woman have been silenced.

With your minds eye focus on the flame and allow everything else to be outside your mind. Allow the vastness to engulf you and do not attach or have any opinions about your experience. At the count of 3 the candle flame will be doused and you will sink into a deep quiet rest. Exhale, pause, and with each breath count;

1, 2, 3.

~J.M.King- Aquarius Agenda~

*

For me when I reach this part of this exercise I move deeply into *Rigpa,* the true nature of mind. This can best be described as a space in which you are not clinging or grasping at an idea or a desire, and not deflecting or pushing away from equally an idea or concept. You are not *doing* anything. At first, treat this as a relaxation space in which you try to maintain periods of *no-thought* . Thoughts may come, allow them to be witnessed and to melt away without any opinion of them- no *attachment* to them. The false self hates rigpa as it shuts him out. It is truly a comfortable place to be in, and when you find it, you will suddenly understand the *why* of meditation. This is the place in which we will carry out our contemplation, in which we implement meditation practices of working towards our eventual release. When we have completed the practice, we will allow it to melt away so that we may remain in stillness. This space of stillness must grow and it will take a little time but this place will eventually become more real and so much bigger and brighter than the outside world. In the mean time the purpose is to quiet the mind and build a single pointed focus on nothingness. Try counting during the focus, when a thought enters, let it melt and start again. While focusing on this nothingness, notice the space between your breath- emptiness. As you breathe in, take in silence from your environment, as you exhale expel your thoughts and or emotional residue.

Here is a focusing exercise to help hone the single pointed concentration capacity. This is your first meditation exercise. This meditation exercise is borrowed from Rudolf Steiners Six Accessory Exercises. This should directly follow your candle meditation. Each meditation requires understanding and absorbing as suggested in your "first lesson". Take 3 to 4 days per meditation before moving on to the next stage, longer is also o.k. Reverting to old meditations as required is also fine. Maintain and let go of them as you see fit.

You are still in the center of the room and all doors and exit points are shut. The outside world is shut off and stillness prevails. This time you stand and walk back towards doorway 1. As you enter you are confronted with the following meditation. (There are ten chapters in this book and the meditations within each chapter correspond to each doorway in the central room.)

Once the candle is doused and you have acclimatized to the space of rigpa, you may approach the door which corresponds to the meditation or chapter you are working on and enter the meditation or contemplation. When you have completed the meditation do not exit quickly. There must be a space of no thought to close the exercise. And take time to emerge from your meditation. Sogyal Rinpoche suggests that a person exiting meditation should behave as one with a severe head wound!

I. Control of Ones Thoughts- meditation

Empty the soul, and then create a simple thought, for example like a brick or a pin. It is better to choose simple, ordinary objects. Tell yourself "I start from this thought, and through my own initiative I will bind with it methodically that which can be connected with the object I have chosen." (this simply means investigate the object thoroughly) When the meditation is completed the vision should be the same as at the beginning- just as vivid. The design of the exercise is to gain control over reflex thought patterns instead of re-playing old tapes of the past, to develop single pointed focus.

~R. Steiner- 6 Complementary Exercises.~

*

Experiment with allowing the pin or brick to be still and then spinning, hovering in the darkness. Try moving back and forwards between spinning and stationary.

Get into the habit of practicing this daily if and when you have a few minutes. With each day the movement of the object should become stronger, easier to summon and more detailed. Do not despair if this takes a little time and try not to force anything. The pin is easier to start with as it is more or less two dimensional in form (less brain work)!

Chapter 2

The Suffering of Change

When the object of your desire has evolved from an exciting, fun, social passtime into a cloud in your mind which is always with you, which has become a parasite that wants everything you ever had, have, or will have, then you come to recognize the suffering of change. This is the true nature of your attachment.

Suffering, in this case, refers to- physical sickness, physical pain and anxieties of the mind. The suffering of change is the recognition that the object of your attachment has evolved from the casual delight that you thought it was in the beginning, into a pervasive, demanding and painful desire. Those of us who are dealing with attachments are dealing with contaminated happiness and that brings suffering. That represents a great many people especially when you include wrong view to be an attachment.

Contaminated happiness is the fake happiness or distraction from reality that we experience when we grab onto our crutch, sex, cigarette or drug of choice. This sort of "happiness" is a poor substitute for the real thing and ironically it always ends in more suffering. The hangover is almost poetic justice. Our attachment and the way we implement it, is just like having

Taurettes syndrome. There is a woman in my village who suffers from Taurettes and everybody avoids her as if she has the plague while she walks down the street cursing and twitching. Cigarette smokers simply light em up and walk on by as if igniting rotting vegetable matter and sucking in the fumes is the most normal thing there is. Both of these actions are reactions to stimulus. If a Taurettes sufferer gets nervous or excited they respond by telling you to fuck off. A smoker lights up in times of anxiety. This means we usually use our attachment to- block out, distract us from or push us away from other things that require our attention, including other forms of suffering. If you don't want to face a problem and tend to ignore it by getting stoned it will only be a bigger problem later. Furthermore you will feel ill-equipped to deal with it while your enduring the hangover or even just the distracting and oppressive status quo of being a daily user of stimulants and or depressants.

It is amazing how small our problems actually are, in fact most of what we call problems as a user simply aren't there when you are sober and fit. Many things we consider problematic when we are users are challenges which you have set yourself previously! A healthy person generally creates a challenging job for himself. If that same person becomes a user of some drug, the exiting, challenging job suddenly becomes a hassle or even too much to handle and suddenly we have gone from mole hill to mountain. Since the thing we are using does not last, or we are forced to stop using it, or we can't afford to use it 24-7, we will have to come down. It generally ends with more suffering, but we half jokingly make appointments with our friends; hey it was fun while it lasted and gee we can do that again as soon as possible...This sort of suffering is the **suffering of change**. What started out as an interesting and fun play thing ends up showing you it's true nature every time. Have you ever picked up a girl or guy and gone home after a heavy nights drinking only to wake up unable to look out of your eyes because of the pain caused by the hangover? If you both feel this way and don't really know each other, generally you could cut the air with a knife in such a situation. Have you honestly reflected on the happy outcome of such a pleasant night out with your attachment and a complete stranger?

Pervasive misery is a persons accumulated mental and physical junk. This comes through karma and negative unpleasant emotions. It is often chronic and can be seen in a persons mental and physical posture. These are things which have weighed on a person for years and are perhaps even carried from a past life. A person suffering pervasive misery can often find solace in the escapism of contaminated happiness and this option seems attractive as it is a genuine easing of suffering or swaping one suffering for another, but it is temporary in nature and is a false "happiness". This sort of happiness would better be described as removing yourself from a grossly unpleasant situation to rest up in a less unpleasant situation. This of course leads to more misery.

Someone suffering from pervasive misery would do well to first segregate themselves from all sorts of triggers and do their best to remain present. All things have their place, even the worst oppression and or suffering must be acknowledged and put in its place otherwise it feeds. Pervasive misery can snowball creating more misery, so if this is you, be mindful of yourself and your triggers. If you find yourself already caught in the trap and are aware of it too late, try to take enough time to reflect, it is good to remember about automated responses and reflex actions spoken of in chapter 1. The first line of defense when we feel the onset of negative emotion, instead of "wallowing in it" and making things worse or "giving in" to it is to simply acknowledge it for what it is and just as you gently brush thoughts aside during meditation, allow them also to be and brush them aside. This is not denial, this is acknowledgment. Escapism is denial.

If we can identify and acknowledge these forms of misery, we can and will learn to fight them.

In fact often recognition of pervasive misery and how we respond to it can start someone off on the road to enlightenment. This event can be one of the two triggers, the one of which shocks people to change their lives. Often after recognizing the true face of our suffering we can become so disgusted that we want to distance ourselves from it in repulsion. This recognition of pervasive suffering along with repulsion and disgust is where the first step of *renunciation in free will* is taken. So your next task is to:

Recognize your suffering and its causes.

All things which are impermanent are changing with every second. You choose which bits you want to identify with all the time, constantly reaffirming your state of I-dentity. At any moment you can choose to dis-I-dentify with or re-create your I-dentity. We do this subconsciously all day and we can consciously implement it as well, and that's an important thing to recognize. Suffering too is impermanent in nature. It too is changing and quite dynamic even now as you read this your suffering and attachments are going through changes. Your attachment and I-dentity there of are constantly being reinforced and broken down by outside influence and are perpetuated or deterred by the responses your mind dishes up. That's why training is required, otherwise you are simply suffering the will-power game and that's far too much hard work! Recognize your suffering though, beit from a hangover/ sick side as well as from the euphoric/ using side. Take a moment to imprint what is actually going on for you.

I say euphoric, this also applies to cigarettes. Everything

written here is always applicable to *all* attachments. Terminology
may differ slightly for a needle, a bad relationship or a fag but the
mechanism is always identical. The psychology and biology are
the same, any illusion a fag smoker may have about being a
different to a "heroin junky" is an exactly that, and I mean no
discredit to the heroin user.

The suffering of change is not a formal meditation but a
recognition of a mechanism which occurs between a human being
unconsciously perpetuating Samsara (cyclic existence) by
repetitively identifying and associating with an object to attain
samsaric or contaminated happiness. The actual suffering part
comes when the human recognizes that the object of his attachment
no longer holds the attractive aspects which drew him in in the first
place however the seduction is no less. In fact the illusion of
seduction and crutch is intimately tied to the mechanism of
attachment which, when it feels threatened seems suddenly
stronger than ever while the side effect of constant attachment
takes its toll physically and mentally. The next step is to up the
dosage and quick! Can you visualize this dreadful connection?
Perhaps, in fact probably definitely, you are in the grip of it right
now!

It would appear I have made a mistake. I wrote that the
object of your attachment no longer holds, but it never held
anything in the first place. That was a lie! At least its contents
never changed. A bottle of wine didn't suddenly acquire some new
ingredient making it more delicious than it was when you were 6
years old. A bottle of wine still has exactly the same ingredients as
a pack of cigarettes, rotting vegetable matter and some fast acting
addictive chemical additives to help speed the delivery of the hit. It
was rubbish when you were 6 and it is the same today.

You haven't changed, you didn't grow an addictive
personality or acquire some chemical imbalance since you were 6

which turned you into a hopeless junky. If society thought they could make more money out of turning you into a carrot or celery junky then we'd all be walking around with poisonous, fast acting vegetables sticking out of our mouths. The suffering of change is very real and we must always seek out the truth, honesty is paramount when dealing with attachments. Two things have happened since you were 6 and they must be recognized and thoroughly understood. In this time the only things that have changed are:

One   :You have been conned!

Two   :That has led to a change in your perspective.

   The fags are the same, the drug is the same, the bottle is the same, the game is the same. The only thing that changes are the players. The unsuspecting idiot steps up to the table and is given his chips. (This is simply going through the motions of *acquiring the perspective* of the drinker/ user/ attached person.) We think we are receiving some right of passage to adulthood and while we don't like the first few hits we know we should stick with it, right of passage and all....Most die as a result of the game. You become a player when your friends start to nudge you towards the evil taboo or it gets administered by a trusted adult who maybe has other plans for you. These players are unfortunately also at the table.

   It doesn't really matter how we got there, the attachment becomes as heavy and hard as set concrete. If we see that the suffering is not something which is of us, that it is not inherent in us, then we have come far. It is of the game, not of us and if we were to stop playing the game, the suffering would quickly stop. Aah but that's the trick right?

   If we take it to the next level, we go even further by

realizing that the object of our desire is *without value to us...* this is important. Now we come to understand that the nature of our desire is *external* and the object of our desire is *of no value*. The logical conclusion is that we are a slave to a conceptualization, a figment of our own imagination.

Right now, understanding that your:

> **desire is not your own and that you do not own it. It does not belong to you. It comes with the game.**

Meditate on the nature of this suffering of change and the nature of your desire. You do not have to achieve anything with this other than the understanding that you have played a part in a game consisting of three parts. A fast acting addictive poison, a victim and a middle man. Supply, demand and profit all revolving around a game (the illusion of desire) in which there are no winners except for the corporation selling you the drug and the government taxing you for being hooked on it.

As you may realize from the opening pages of this chapter, our perspective has become something which we must always be prepared to question, especially on this road. If we could go through life without having to make opinions about everything the world would be a friendlier place. Then we would see our world as a collection of precepts instead of concepts.

*The minute we add **concept** into the equation we have added all the baggage of our **I-dentity** onto it.*

*

What can I do with this, my attachment is too big to conquer! How does all this philosophizing improve or impede my chances of controlling my attachment?

Try this analogy; I really need to fix that leak in the roof, in no time the sun and rain will be getting in and damaging the woodwork, I must get call the repair guy or climb up there my self. The leak should be dealt with and forgotten about. It only becomes a problem when we do nothing about it and the wood work starts to suffer. If we still do nothing about it, it grows in our mind until we are thinking of nothing else. "My god the woodwork is so damaged I can stick my finger through the wall, if I don't do something soon the rain will start pouring in and the carpets will get damaged...The job that was so small appears to be getting bigger and the consequences more serious, but still we don't act. We close the door to that room and pretend it's not there, if we don't look it might go away... right? This buys us a short amount of time but the damage is now simply out of sight and while this may temporarily put the effects of the neglect out of our mind, the problem has now become chronic and we are in a state of denial.

Now our problem (which is not really a problem but due to the nature of the game we have allowed it to become "in our life") has become enormous. What if I was to visit you and tell you that it wasn't actually that bad, all you have to do is climb up on the roof and replace *one broken roof tile*. This will stop the rain coming in and hence any further damage. Sure the damage you have allowed to build up till now has to be repaired but that is just a question of a little time and elbow grease. The only problem you ever had was one small crack in a roof tile. As a precept this means very little, as your concept (I-dentity plus all the baggage that brings) it seems bigger than mount Everest!

The important thing to take with you out of this is of course the question of perspective. The actual replacing of the roof tile is the simplest thing and takes 5 minutes. Our I-dentity and baggage are the reasons we fail to do this, not that the content of the cigarette or wine bottle or line of coke has any secret ingredient making it desirable beyond measure and not because of an addictive personality which suddenly became activated when we turned fifteen. If you could see the object of your attachment as rain and the replacing of the roof tile as the cure *and* could simply implement this into your life, then our work would be done. In reality it is this simple.

If I Google <u>precept</u> this is what I get:

- *a commandment or direction given as a rule of action or conduct.*

- *An injunction as to moral conduct; maxim.*

- *A procedural directive or rule, as for the performance of some technical operation.*

   If I look up <u>concept</u> I get the following:

- *A general notion or idea; conception.*

- *An idea of something formed by mentally combining all its characteristics or particulars; a construct.*

- *A directly conceived or intuited object of thought.*

   It is very important to be able to differentiate between what is concept and what is precept, almost no one does this. The thing is we walk among precepts all day long and we treat them as concepts. Our mind made reality (or I-dentity-consciousness) relies upon turning precepts into concepts, all day long it is making an inventory of everything it sees and processing it. This is great when trying to light a fire with a piece of flint or some such thing but not when you are trying to re-construct reality according to you. You are noy god! This is an important issue to wrap your head around, I-dentity, creating attachments through conceptualizing precepts. It does this because it is trying to make sense of the world around it and it is defending its own very existence, it has become self-aware if you like. The mind gaining an I-dentity becomes self-aware and at that point it takes over the show while it is supposed to be a tool, not judge, jury and executioner.

This is the reason we don't remember much of anything before a certain age, we were living in the moment and without I-dentity until the mind awoke unto itself and placed itself above biology and firmly in the driver seat. Now it will do anything to avoid being found out which means it will fight with you during this chapter. A precept is everything we come in contact with, call it phenomena if you like. A concept is heralded by an emotion which signifies the identification we give to a precept. Its truth becomes clouded to us because of our perspective,

How can this help me control my drug intake?

Very mixed up stuff don't you agree, everything appears to be a lie! As a concept, your mind has robbed the object of its own I-dentity and made it part of its own mental make up. This is how we turn "water into wine" or poison into something to be coveted. Get into the habit of reminding yourself that the object you are getting excited about during your day is a precept not a concept. Experiment with recognizing the absurdity of your personal view of things in your daily life. I recognize it if I go to the supermarket. The section where the alcoholic drinks were sold would always have a pull or attraction, especially if I was toying with the idea of cutting down. I would even be busy with it before I went to the shop. Now days I have three bottles of wine and one of hard liquor in the cupboard in case friends come over and they mean absolutely nothing to me. (the alcohol I mean). Simple, concept is now precept.

Many of us have at some point in our lives given up sugar in our tea or coffee or we have witnessed someone who has done this. Usually, at some point, the quitter forgets that they have given up and or someone serves them a coffee and forgets that they have stopped with the sugar. If this has happened to you, you will understand immediately what I mean. The person will spit the coffee on the floor in disgust. What was a once a pleasure and not to be drunk any other way only two weeks ago has become as poison to the taste. This is how quickly the brain adjusts to change, the mind is the only trouble maker and needs a good beating now and then!

This point is not to make you feel uncomfortable about having to deal with the mind until it gets used to "no sugar", this is making the point about precept and concept valid. The mind we will deal with, it will be painless by the time you are ready to quit. If we see the roof tile and the poison as precepts (which is all they are in the real world) our attachment to them becomes laughable. Sorry, I know it's hard to say that, and your attachment is to be taken very seriously... until you look at it from the other side, then I promise you, you will laugh out loud. Behind door number two are the following meditations; Suffering of Change & Right View.

Suffering of change- meditation

Do you love the thing you crave?

Your devotion until now has been absolute.

You cannot imagine life with out it.

It is your crutch in times of need.

It is often all you think about until you are allowed to

be with it again.

But what is it that you actually hold so dear?

Your devotion to it leaves no time or will for

anything of value,

It has been allowed to creep into

every aspect of your life,

It cuts you down so that it can half way prop you up again.

Many have lived and died thinking of nothing other

than this illusion with no intrinsic value what so ever.

Do you love your attachment?

Do you see it?

*

There's a lot to take in in this chapter and there's an important element which ties the rest together and helps you close this second section. It is the nature of impermanence and imperfection. This is one of the most important aspects of Buddhist understanding and it is definitely a cornerstone of meditation practices and comprehension of the true nature of things. The concept comes forth in the meditation "Right View" mentioned directly so now is a good time to broach it. Right view is the first step of 8 on the Wheel of Dharma.

For our purposes, the understanding of the impermanence and imperfection of all things is relevant because if it is understood, you will comprehend that;

Not one thing is without an ending!...
But everything gets re-used!

This goes for all ideology, trees and cars, Christianity, Buddhism and the empire state building. And **your vision of your own habit!** Eventual there will be no sign that the human race was ever here, not even old bones. In time all things turn to dust *and are re-used.* All things of the world of form vanish as do our concepts. All the rules and codes of conduct vanish. Everything we held dear or thought was cool.

It seems to be a paradox, we have so much with regard to form and "freedom". At least we have the opportunity to gather as much form as we desire, but we can't take it with us and we can't use it all up before we go. Just as we are all busy adhering to codes of conduct and ideology, but what happens to that when we are gone? Nothing? It never was? To what was it ever something?

I am reminded of a piece by Rudolf Steiner which may be of some help in illustrating the elusive, formless spark which *is* life or the basis energy of emptiness moving from form to formless as something dies or something is born, indifferent to duality. It also illustrates how much more important our connection to the formless aspect is than the in our face form based reality.

Within manifested nature the physical body, according to occult science, is that part of man which is of the same nature as that of the mineral kingdom. On the other hand, that which distinguishes man from minerals is considered as not being part of the physical body. From the occult point of view, what is of supreme importance is the fact that death separates the human being from that which, during life, is of like nature with the mineral world. Occult science points to the dead body as that part of man which is to be found existing in the same way in the mineral kingdom. It lays strong emphasis upon the fact that in this principle of the human being, which it looks upon as the physical body, and which death reduces to a corps, the same minerals and forces are at work as in the mineral realm; but no less emphasis is laid upon the fact that at death disintegration of the physical body sets in. Occult science therefore states "It is true that the same materials and forces are at work in the physical body as in the mineral world but during life their activity is placed at the disposal of something higher. They are left to themselves only when death occurs. Then they act, as they must in conformity with their own nature, as decomposer's of the physical body.

~Rudolf Steiner- a Philosophy of Freedom~

*

It is this spark of life that is the issue, the truth of it all. The spark which is our life line to ultimate truth. The spark which we may carry for a while is a representation of this ultimate truth. When we die it simply retreats from the body, its vehicle on this side. It is the same life that is in all things!We shouldn't take this thing called life so personally. Saying things like

"this is my life"

is a very peculiar statement when observed from this perspective. Suddenly we see it as a view point held by a fictitious character who has no substance in the world of form or the formless. Our I-dentity is not even the same as the version of "us"carried around by our closest loved one. Our I-dentity is nothing more than one idea in our own head which holds power over all things by tricking the mind into being its slave. Our I-dentity is nothing more than a fictitious avatar! This is the same trick as that activated by our attachments.

Awareness is the first step in our evolution. Remaining in a sort of gridlock of the mind keeps humanity stuck in all the bad stuff. We need to ask ourselves while I am here in this body, what is the information I can use to make the world a better place for my children as opposed to what are the things which support stale ideology and maintain dysfunction and corruption in the world. This sounds too big to have anything to do with your attachment but it has everything to do with it.

We have created our way, or I-dentity, our code of likes and dislikes, do's and don't s, good and bad, the way we look out through our eyes at the world. This will all vanish without a trace the moment we die. The only thing that there is which actually *is*, is this moment and every moment until we die. Karma will visit us to let us know if we are making the right choices in life or the wrong ones. The best thing we could do with the time we have is listen to our karma, because one day very soon time will run out and it's the choices we make which represent our life, nothing more. Any discussion about what is good or bad for us is merely ourselves at war with ourselves, the gridlock of dualistic thought. When we are stuck in dualistic thought we go no where quickly.

We live as biological quantum computers constantly probing incoming information and reacting to the signals, this means our identity is constantly being presented with the opportunity to change our reality or remain as we are. Our only malfunction comes through faulty administrators who running the show by sorting the incoming information. When these guys start to argue, we are suffering from what is commonly known as Schizophrenia. People suffering from attachments are Schizophrenic. The attachment is the spanner in the works which causes confusion for the administrator. The good news is that this vanishes as soon as one dies.... *or as soon as the individual realizes his ability to change his I-dentity at any moment.*

To comprehend this and be trained to the point that you can get rid of these I-dentity flaws rapidly and painlessly is akin to a quantum leap in your evolution. It is quite possible that with out meditation you would have lived a radically different life. This has the power to greatly impact the lives of everyone you care about and the way you interact with them.

(The further you read the more sense the meditations will make. If there are some area's you find vague or feel you don't really understand, leave it alone, it will become obviouse in time.)

Right View- meditation

This is simply the start and finish of the path, it means to see things as they are as one complete. As such, right view is the cognitive aspect of wisdom. **It means to see through things, to grasp the impermanent and imperfect nature of worldly objects and ideas, and to understand the law of karma and karmic conditioning.** *Right view has very little to do with any intellectual capacity, just as wisdom is not just a matter of intelligence. Instead, right view is attained, sustained, and enhanced through all capacities of mind. It begins with the intuitive insight that all beings are subject to suffering and it ends with complete understanding of the true nature of all things. <u>Since right perception of the world forms our thoughts and our actions, right view will deliver right thoughts and right actions</u>. Our essence must relearn this view making it part of our reflex drive.*

~Wheel of Dharma~

*

Be mindful of the fact that karma is deeply tied in with cause and effect, programming and conditioning. Change in cause alters the effect but a conscious change in the effect can also alter the cause. The more removed one is from the immediate circle of influence the more watered down the mechanism. Through wisdom, acceptance and meditation, effect can adjust cause, even over lifetimes. The true nature of things refers to the lack of intrinsic self, their emptiness of a self established through identification and conceptualization. It also refers to the shared bond of a common life force, a unity among sentient beings. More about this later.

(practical exercise)

Control of ones Action- Exercise.

Take on a simple task like caring for a plant. Basil always needs looking after! Be present while doing it. Make sure that you are taking care of the plant in the true sense, for example watering regularly and removing dead leaves so that the plant does not waste energy. One at a time add new tasks, new altruistic projects, or simply new plants. DO NOT become attached to the process, it is simply your directive.

~R. Steiner- 6 Complementary Exercises.~

*

While caring for this plant be mindful of the fact that the same essence or life force which is in you resides in this plant. Just as you desire happiness and freedom from suffering, so does this plant, as its ideal opportunity for growth. You are responsible for its well being or demise. Be mindful of cause and effect, be also mindful of the effect the plant now has on you.

Chapter 3

Liberation of Compassion

*What do they mean, those guys on T.V. survival shows when
they say;"Your best asset in a survival situation is a positive
frame of mind"? The statement insinuates that perspective
(formless) has more to offer than our actions (form)?*

Thought has the power to hold up an illusion of I-dentity
and reality for most people from the time they become self aware
(I-dentity aware) until the time they die. In principal there is
nothing wrong with this, it is a bit like a group of people on a
sinking ship, a leader will automatically stand up and passengers
will follow him as their best bet for survival. The trouble is this
reluctant leader (our ego, false self, what ever you want to call it)
is manifested in our time of need and cultivated by authority
figures to fit in to Samsara, so we have a take charge figure trained
to take care of number one, trying to bend reality to fit his
expectations, the result of his programming. It's a bit like Brad Pits
character in the film Fight Club. He plays the part of a fictitious
person who takes over from the host played by Edward Norton
when he can't cope with his reality. Very charming, very capable,
just not real and in the end extremely destructive when placed in
everyday situations. For better or worse, out of all the primordial
ooze of our first years, we prepare this take charge (or perpetuate

failure) creature and lay in waiting for just for the right moment to implement him. We wait until we we're confronted with a situation, for just the right opportunity, then we activate him. It probably starts with goo goo da da ma ma. We watch with glee as our parents praised the thing that they, in their wisdom, have created. *We* have done well! And now you will literally have to kill him to get rid of him. Just like the film!

Our I-dentity, while merely a *figment of our imagination*, has a lot of power as do our thoughts when directed towards an external object. Remember Dr Emoto's water experiments? He placed water from a polluted river in a freezer and water from a pure clean lake next to it and had miraculous results. When he observed the crystals one was beautiful and the other literally disfigured. He went further placing hateful names and or words on others, playing aggressive music while conducting the opposite test in the room next door acquiring even more astounding results.

Realizing how powerful the thought construct of our I-dentity is, and taking Emoto's experiments on board as evidence of what thought can do, one can't help but realize that while it is unseen and not of the world of form, these quiet, invisible energies seem to posses more power than the stuff of matter. Try it, the one thing you absolutely can not deny is the illusion of your self, until you know better and even then the voice will creep back into your head the moment you let your guard down. History is littered with the refuse of I-dentity recognition as the self;

"I think therefore I am"

The same stuff which is responsible for the re-construction of these water crystals travels *the same road* to the people you meet and correspond with every day. Needless to say they too are also 70% water. This means you are an important link in the chain of events which either spreads the energy of Lake

Biwako or Lake Shimanto to your colleagues and fellow human beings.

Water before Prayer   Water after Prayer

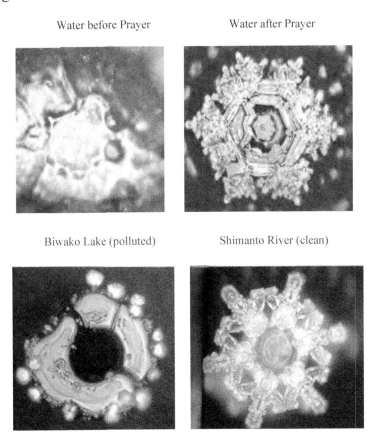

Biwako Lake (polluted)   Shimanto River (clean)

    While you are the one suffering, you might find it difficult to embrace the notion of compassion for others at this point in time. Not that you are actually suffering, but you are busy with the notion that you are about to undertake something enormous and that it will be the struggle of your life etc, etc. Forgive me for playing it down, but you haven't actually stopped doing anything yet so you are not suffering from anything except an idea about something that might happen in the future, and of course the usual hum of being a substance abuser. I say might because you may not finish this book which means; might. If you finish it, and follow the instructions you will stop. I have no control over you actually finishing but I hope you do. I hope so because I wish that every human could experience what I have experienced. I am talking about quitting attachments but also about waking up to life.

One of the main reasons we need to develop and maintain a sense of compassion toward others is because it travels. We investigate compassion because it is healthy for all, we can expirience its benefits and pass them on to others. As a user, we have lost touch with true compassion, it is mired by I-dentification. I read an interesting interview with the Dalai Lama in which he was discussing the nature of compassion as a selfish act. His claim was that one should behave in a compassionate manner *for his own benefit!* He even went so far to give it a name; *"selfish compassion"*. Through compassionate acts, we start to cultivate another aspect of our selves which does not get so much attention in our society. This blind spot creates a wall of separation between us and our fellow man. Humans are by nature social animals, it is just that we have created a way of life which supports territoriality and segregation as the standard posture thus widening the gulf between us and those outside our social circles.

We now know that co-operation in nature is the way of progress, evolution and survival. Things tend to work together to overcome obsticals than to go it alone. Single celled organisms even worked out that if they join together and delegated tasks to different groups of cells they were much more effective than flying solo. My theory is if you can use it for a positive outcome then grab it with both hands. This is so of compassion in that subtle changes in our posture towards our fellow man will quickly and dramatically change the feedback we get from our fellows and environment. If you smile at someone you have just met they are going to be much more open to possitive interaction than if you grimace at them, regardless of their intention.

York University study finds small acts of kindness have big impact on emotional well-being.

TORONTO, May 17, 2011 –Practicing small acts of kindness will make you a happier person, and the boost in mood stays with you for months, according to research out of York University.

More than 700 people took part in a study which charted the effects of being nice to others, in small doses, over the course of a week. Researchers asked participants to act compassionately towards someone for 5-15 minutes a day, by actively helping or interacting with them in a supportive and considerate manner. Six months later, participants reported increased happiness and self-esteem.

"The concept of compassion and kindness resonates with so many religious traditions, yet it has received little empirical evidence until recently," says lead author Myriam Mongrain, associate professor of psychology in York's Faculty of Health. "What's amazing is that the time investment required for these changes to occur is so small. We're talking about mere minutes a day," she says.

Participants' levels of depression, happiness, and self-esteem were assessed at the study's onset, and at four subsequent points over the following six months; those in the compassionate condition reported significantly greater increases in self-esteem and happiness at six months compared to those in the control group.

So why does doing good for others make us feel good about ourselves?

"The simplest answer is that doing noble, charitable acts make us feel better about ourselves. We reaffirm that we are 'good,' which is a highly-valued trait in our society. It is also possible that being kind to others may help us be kind to ourselves," Mongrain says. She notes that previous studies have demonstrated a causal relationship between compassionate behaviors and charitable self-evaluations.

{"Compassion cuts both ways," she says. "If you make a conscious decision to not be so hard on others, it becomes easier to not be so hard on yourself.}

Furthermore, providing support to others often means that we will get support back. That is why caring for and helping others may be the best possible thing we can do for ourselves. On a less selfish level, there is something intrinsically satisfying about helping others and witnessing their gratitude," says Mongrain.

Not surprisingly, research has also shown that compassionate activities increase the level of meaning in one's life, which in turn elevates levels of happiness.

Researchers expected that those with needy personalities would experience greater reductions in depressive symptoms and greater increases in happiness and self-esteem as a result of being kind to others.

"We hypothesized this would occur as a result of the reassurance [needy personalities] might extract from positive exchanges with others," Mongrain says. "We did see some reduction in depressive symptoms for anxiously attached individuals, but further research is needed to see if there is any long-term benefit."

The study, "Practicing Compassion Increases Happiness and Self-Esteem," is forthcoming in the spring issue of the Journal of Happiness Studies. It is co-authored by York University researchers Jacqueline Chin and Leah Shapira. The research was funded by the Social Sciences and Humanities Research Council of Canada (SSHRC).

York University is the leading interdisciplinary research and teaching university in Canada. York offers a modern, academic experience at the undergraduate and graduate level in Toronto, Canada's most international city. The third largest university in the country, York is host to a dynamic academic community of 50,000 students and 7,000 faculty and staff, as well as 200,000 alumni worldwide. York's 10 Faculties and 28 research centers conduct ambitious, groundbreaking research that is interdisciplinary, cutting across traditional academic boundaries. This distinctive and collaborative approach is preparing students for the future and bringing fresh insights and solutions to real-world challenges. York University is an autonomous, not-for-profit corporation.

As we start to understand the true nature of phenomena as a precept and can clearly see the difference between precept and concept, the nature of the I-dentity of objects in relation to ourselves indeed our own I-dentity, we are forced to ask ourselves the same questions about our fellow man. If we close ourselves off from others outside our social circles, we are giving these faceless millions no name or I-dentity whether it be grosser or subtler self, true or false. This *concept* of strangers robs them of not only their own I-dentity or sovereignty in our eyes but also of their basic humanity. In our version of Samsaric reality we choose to live among strangers with no name or face or I-dentity. More sinister than this is the current climate of propaganda which tells us that strangers or those who are "different" are actually terrorist bogeymen! This mechanism, which we are trying to reverse through meditation, knowledge and wisdom, is actually promoted to insight fear as a form of control. This is the current posture of the first worlder towards his fellow man. I recently traveled from winter in a busy part of Holland to mid summer in semi-rural Australia and back again. It seems the better the weather in combination with the more rural environment makes for a much more positive social interaction among strangers. This holds true even though the current Australian government is anti-Muslim and opportunistically jumping on the band wagon of Ebola to stop *any* "undesirables" entering the country. The sickness is still there, there are an awful lot of conservative folk in Australia, but it would appear that the less people stacked up on top of each other the lesser the problem of social paralysis. By cutting others off and not wanting interaction unless it is absolutely necessary we are, as social animals, doing ourselves a dis-service and denying *our own* humanity.

As you might imagine, building higher and higher walls around ourselves only exacerbates our social identity sickness. Emotions, postures and concepts belonging to this sickness are things like territoriality, racism, paranoia, ignorance, fear, envy. Social separation doesn't deliver any positive emotions. These negative emotions are also one of the main reasons we reach for the defense mechanism. These are moments in which a subconscious signal is being sent from the brain to the hand by-passing all regulatory aspects. And the worst thing of all is that this is a chronic and permanent status quo, a depressive norm with swings toward deeper depression and it is so normal we don't even know it anymore, the uneasy hum of modern life...

Our next hurdle is one of realizing comparison and identification. The minute you start to open yourself to another, there are elements of comparison and identification spoken of in chapter 1. These are things of Samsara and the false self and should be gently brushed aside and replaced with genuine interest for the other person. This is where compassion comes in. If you have truly *cultivated* compassion then this interest is automatic and not feigned (more about this later). It is the comparison and identification rubbish which makes you feel uneasy, not the interaction with a member of the same species. It is at times like these that we can reflect upon the words of the Dalai Lama;

"We are all searching for happiness and want to avoid suffering."

In fact if we can look beyond the false, illusive I-dentity sitting across from us and look beyond the nature of desires (also a thing of I-dentity), eventually if you can peel away all the layers, all you are left with is life staring back at you through another vehicle. We expirience this as recognizing a kindred spirit and in principal that's exactly what we are doing except we are recognizing *the* kindred spirit. Is it not so then, that all we want to do is join with the other in recognition and celebration of life? We all know that moment when we have looked in the eyes of another and seen life itself looking back and smiling, with no defenses raised. These are the moments when we tend to recognize a bond and label it true friendship or love but what we are actually doing is lowering our guard and corresponding openly. These are the true resources of this planet. It's not about fossil fuels or solar energy, it's not about duality, good and evil, it is about collective human consciousness waking up to itself and moving on in the only way there is to go forward. In compassion and with loving kindness. Anything else is just a game of musical chairs which causes the lack of equality among us because there will always be some kluts left high and dry with his pants down around his ankles when the music stops.

This notion of equality for all sentient beings is crucial for our own awakening, for our own true I-dentity and for the cessation of our madness.

A persons general sense of goodness is in direct correlation to the kind of thoughts he or she generates. Dogs express great joy and delight when they see people of good nature. Conversely, those who are of ill will are regarded with suspicion. Therefore a kind motivation or a kind heart is an extremely valuable quality and of the utmost importance for positive growth. People who posses compassion are amiable to all and their nature is attractive to all. When somebody smiles for example, it creates joy in other peoples hearts for free.

HOW do we meditate on compassion and equanimity?

On one hand we must develop **compassion towards all suffering beings**, and secondly we must **identify the nature of suffering**. If we examine the state of our ordinary minds, we may see how the mind will separate people into three groups

- loved ones ~ open and friendly posture,

- enemies ~ ill-will, and

- strangers ~ indifference.

Analise your feelings towards these three groups. In truth, as far as we are concerned, our compassion toward others is one sided and superficial as it is primarily, in an unconscious person, viewed through the eyes of the I-dentity,

"what's in it for me"?

This is also the case when we look at our attitude towards the three groups mention above. Therefore in order to cultivate true compassion for *all* beings, we must first develop an attitude of equality, an impartial thought that views all all beings equally.

(If you could understand the notion of the selflessness of all people, which you will understand before this book is done,

you would understand instantly that equality and compassion for your enemy is a given as his viewpoint is ultimately a question of attachment and identity, quite simply put, he is you.)

We come to realize that the while we feel close to our relatives and friends and we behave in a compassionate manner towards them, this comes from a space of attachment and clinging. A selfish motive is behind our apparent kindness. We have made a deal with this relative/ friend that requires a code of behavior and while we follow this code, our bond could more accurately be called attachment.

Equanimity- meditation material

Concentrate on particular individuals. Choose three, one who has harmed you, one who is your enemy, and one to whom you are indifferent.

While concentrating on your enemy, the mind thinks; "here is my enemy"and becomes dark and heavy, hateful.

Think about your friend. How does the mind feel now?

And now the stranger to whom you have probably a neutral reaction.

Why do I feel this way about these individuals? Analise it, are the reasons narrow and self serving in nature?

None of these people were born our friends or enemies. We are positively interested in our friends because of benefits they have brought us and our enemies have a similar relationship to us. That is all action and reaction. Relationships built on such ground are unstable and unreliable. Only relationships built on a foundation of love and genuine compassion are stable and reliable. These are called unconditional.

~Stages of meditation- HH the Dalai Lama~

*

One of my so-called best friends stopped having contact with me when I stopped drinking and playing music for a living. (I was a professional musician for 30 years). I thought we would be friends to the death but apparently that was it. He is headstrong and I could imagine in another set of circumstances we would have made great enemies! Circumstances change and now he is somebody with whom I have simply no contact. This happens when people stop work or move away, it's not as if you will lose valuable friends when you stop drinking or smoking or whatever. They were simply over rated, perhaps you could even call them Samsaric friends. This is a perfect exsample of the two truths at work, relative and ultimate. And as far as getting whacked together, laughing together about something that's not even funny does not constitute having a great time, that's an illusion. These are the "friends" we make in this place of purgatory.

They are merely partners in crime.

Our best friend can turn into our worst enemy tomorrow. And a much hated enemy can turn into a most trusted friend. Our animosity towards enemies and attachment towards friends merely exhibits a narrow minded attitude that can only see some temporary or fleeting advantage. Viewed from a broader perspective we come to see the futility of clinging to desire and other nonsensical emotions like hatred and hostility.

Believing in reincarnation simplifies this notion. The two root causes for being born into Samara and the cause of Samsara itself are Karma and disturbing emotions. Through our ignorance and lack of ability to learn from our mistakes we are forced to come back if you like, so that we may have another shot at it. This is the nature of cyclic existence. This means also that everyone we know has at some time been our friend, enemy and stranger. Everyone of them has benefited us directly or indirectly. The kindness and benefit of our friends and relatives is quite obvious in this life due to the notion that we have a code and will support each other-*in this life*. It is logical then that we should maintain the same posture towards all beings remembering their kindness to us in previous lives. Coming to truly understand this constitutes a phase recognized in Buddhism as the **awakening mind of bodhichitta**. This means that the mind has realized this wisdom and is prepared to implement it as a new, personal reality. Through generation of compassion you generate merit for yourself at the bank of karma but also on the physical plane. That traveling Emoto energy goes with you and the more you generate positive energy towards your fellow man, the more merit you are creating. All beings are important to us in the accumulation of merit, you could say that your enemies are of immense value to you as they offer great opportunities for growth and merit.

This is why we need to try to generate compassion towards our fellow man. It is a form of paying it forward.

Morality of Individual Liberation-

Exercise to be read before meditations

* you may need to write these out on a larger piece of paper and place them before you so that you can read them during meditation. At least write key words so that you can continue with the least distraction. Read what you need to read then relax back into meditation. I find memorizing the main theme of each step to be the best approach as it is less disturbing for your balance during meditation though if your mind is fuddled with the burden of attachment this may be difficult.

1/   *Examine your motivation as often as you can. Even before getting out of bed in the morning, establish a nonviolent, non-abusive outlook for your day. At night examine, how you have conducted yourself during the day.*

2/   *Notice how much suffering there is in your own life.*

    1. *There is physical and mental pain which you naturally seek to avoid, such as sickness, hangovers, aging, and death.*

    2. *There are temporary experiences, like eating good food and drink that seems to be pleasurable in and of themselves but, if partaken continuously, turn into pain- this is the suffering of change. When a situation switches from pleasure to pain, reflect on the fact that the deeper nature of the original pleasure is revealing itself. Attachment to such superficial pleasures will only bring you more pain.*

    3. *Reflect on how you are caught in a general process of conditioning that rather than being under your control,*

you are trapped under the influence of karma and afflictive emotions.

3/   *Gradually develop a realistic view of the body through examining its constituents, skin, blood, flesh, and so forth.*

4/   *Analise your life closely. You will eventually find it difficult to misuse it by becoming machinelike or by merely seeking money or mentaly and physically incapacitiating yourself as a surrogate for happiness.*

5/   *Adopt a positive attitude in the face of difficulty. Imagine that by undergoing a difficult situation you are also undermining worse consequences from other karma's that you would otherwise have to experience in the future. As a mental exercise, take upon yourself the burden of everyone's suffering of that type.*

6/   *Evaluate the possible negative and positive effects of feelings such as lust, anger, jealousy, and hatred. When it becomes obvious that their effects are harmful, you will have arrived at the conclusion that there are no positive results of, say anger. Analyze more and more, and gradually your conviction will strengthen; repeated reflection on the disadvantages of anger will cause you to realize that it is senseless, and even pathetic. This decision will cause your anger to gradually diminish. The same is true of desire for the object of your attachment.*

7/   *Having recognized the scope of suffering, research its cause, and identify that the source of suffering is ignorance of the true nature of persons and things, and that lust, hatred, and so forth are based on this ignorance. Realize that suffering can be removed, can be extinguished into the sphere of reality. Reflect that this true cessation is attained by the practice of morality, concentrated meditation, and wisdom- true paths.*

8/ *Notice your attachment to food, clothes, and shelter, and experiment with adapting monastic practices of contentment to a lay person's life. Be satisfied with adequate food, clothing and shelter. Use the additional free time for meditation so that you can overcome more problems.*

9/ *Develop a strong wish to refrain from doing harm to other, either physically or verbally, no matter whether you are embarrassed, insulted, reviled, pushed or hit.*

~How to Practise- HH the Dalai Lama~

*

Morality of Concern for Others- meditation

Perform the 5 step visualization for developing compassion.

1/   Remain calm and reasonable.

2/   In front of you to the right, imagine another version of yourself, egotistical and self centered. He has an entire wing of this building just for himself and all the stock piles of bread he keeps receiving. They are going moldy because no one ever eats them but due to the fact that the egotistical version of yourself receives them, he has power and can sit in his armchair and revel in his attachments all day long.

3/   In front of you and to the left, imagine a group of poor people, suffering people who are unrelated to you, neither friend or enemy. These people are starving and need bread. They suffer no attachments but are truly suffering of starvation because the bread always gets given to the egotistical version of you who is now sniffing cocaine and grinning stupidly as AC/DC starts blaring through the prison.

4/   Observe these two sides from your calm vantage point. Now think, "Both want happiness. Both want to get rid of suffering. Both have the right to accomplish these goals."

5/   Consider this: Just as usually we are prepared to make temporary sacrifices for a greater long term good, so the benefit of the larger number of suffering beings to your left is much more important than the single egotistical person on your right. Further more the egotistical version of you has no real need, he is in the grip of madness, still he requires those in need to go with out, even die just to maintain his illusions. Notice your mind naturally turning to the side of the greater number of people. This reflex morality must be taken with you into the real world.

~How to Practise- HH the Dalai Lama~

*

Equanimity in Feeling- exercise

Maintain balance at all times between sorrow and joy, do not delve in ecstasy or extremes in either direction. Notice the impulse for this when it arises and counter it. Try to maintain inner peace and stillness.

~R. Steiner- 6 Complementary Exercises.~

*

* Of course the above exercise doesn't count for the times when you are using. You are expected to continue using until you have finished the book.

Chapter 4

Thought Palace & Hungry Ghosts

Hungry ghosts are pitiable creatures with huge, empty stomachs. They have pinhole mouths, and their necks are so thin they cannot swallow, so they remain hungry. Beings are reborn as hungry ghosts because of their greed, envy and jealousy. Hungry ghosts are also associated with addiction, obsession and compulsion.

In this chapter I would like for us to build a foundation. We are going to build three elements into one concept that will stand solid as an oak. These three are:

- *Thought Palace*: A mental space which is a constant to where you may retreat or simply take strength and or recuperate.

- *Defects and Antidotes*: to problems that occur during meditation

- *Tools and Weapons:* to combat the monsters we are going to deal with.

But first, who is this administrator in your head and at what time is the changing of the guard? Who is on shift when I reach for a drink or fag or a line of coke? It is certainly not the same guy who is running the show at 3.30 am when I wake up groping in the dark for water to quench my thirst and transform this thing in my mouth from a belt sander back into a tongue. I am sure that you have experienced this paradox during the course of your attachment career. While part of you is asking these questions, another part of you is egging you on! The times you allow yourself to partake are on the increase and the border of *when is it appropriate to do so* is becoming increasingly vague. This is already a conflict of interests which only confirms that there are more than one of you. As the space between hits becomes shorter the psychological and physical pressure applied directly by your attachment has made it more difficult to control. Your attachment along with this rogue administrator has become akin to a sort of dynamic entity or, as Dexter would call it, a dark passenger, all powerful on the one hand and skulking in shame, timid as a mouse at other times.

The administrators point of view is crucial and this is where the schizophrenia comes in. He is the guy who let's us down with things like "Mwaa o.k., Just one then", as if it's o.k. to be a little bit pregnant! And how could two adverse perspectives abide in the same body when their opinions are so opposed to each other? It's quite straight forward, just as our body tells us when we need to eat, our body tells us that our drug level in the blood is dropping. That's the physical side of it, the psychological aspect goes hand in hand with the physical. Often when coming down, we expirience the uneasiness of our mind caused by the drug. To increase our terror, we must endure the paranoia caused by blackouts and memory loss, the inevitable side effects of heavy abuse, at least with alcohol and many hard drugs. Oddly enough, after all this torture and punishment, we still believe that we find certain aspects of this fictitious character (you while under the influence) to be things we hold dear and, from an I-dentity point of view, crucial aspects of our make up! It's like a bad relationship,

"I know he hits me when he's drunk but he's always sorry and he never really means it. He's so sweet when he's sober."

There are *no* redeeming factors and any positive traits you imagine him to posses, you posses already. If you were to quit all you have to do is keep what you like and jettison what you don't. Once more the only issue here is one of I-dentity and cognitive dissonance with the added disorientation of coming down. You will still be there after you quit! Any compromise like this would be looked upon as extremely unhealthy by a relationship therapist. Furthermore, if you could record yourself getting drunk or high you would probably find those redeeming factors to be not worth it after all. Even cigarette smoking viewed from the perspective of a non-smoker is revolting and singularly unattractive, perhaps worse than watching a drunk do his thing. The only things you will lose by quitting attachments are:

things you will not miss.

We do however have one advantage, this administrator works for us! This means we determine what he thinks and does, not him, we just forget it sometimes and throw him the keys. Humans have a tendency to let their administrator run the show whether they are talking (90% is worthless information), shopping, having a shower. It's called auto pilot, not being present and this is a very suggestive state to be in which is what advertising cartels rely upon. We also have the ability to be influenced by our surroundings and friends, certainly this is dangerous when on auto pilot. Meditation is all about disciplining the mind to deal with exactly this sort of trouble so that situations which would normally waken the hungry ghost in us will no longer trigger that reaction. From a psychological point of view we have some killin to do.

1/ Thought Palace-important exercise

You need to cultivate a thought palace which is like a concrete tower in your mind, unbreakable and impenetrable. Thoughts come in two forms, **contrived** and **reflex**. Contrived thought is the one we choose to implement and can develop. Once we have built in the contrived thought through repetitive exercise during meditation, it becomes part of us, then we are on the way to creating new healthy reflex thought. This is about building new reflex reactions to stimulus. New thoughts are either derived at by new information or conscious effort to implement something you are not at home with. Contrived thoughts always come before reflex thought, even programming starts as contrived or copied information. To design our new contrived thought we first have to decide what it is we are trying to achieve. I will offer some points:

- renunciation of our negative emotions and attachments

- denial of the illusion of desire

- freedom, peace and restfulness

These three things will form the basis of our mindset while visiting our thought palace. Since our natural posture of mind is to conceptualize everything we are going to use this against it! Our thought palace is going to rise out of a reconstruction of our starter's meditation which you should by now be using daily. In this meditation we are going to place a room behind door number 6. *This will also be the room with the leaky roof tile discussed earlier. Our thought palace will start life as a contrived idea.

(Remember in the starter's meditation or candle meditation, there are 10 entry points to the central room? Some are doors, some are windows and you have to close them off one by one. As the entry ways are closed or curtains are drawn the outside world (our thoughts) are quietened. This meditation is the one I use which is based on an actual house belonging to a relative who always has sick people staying with her. They always stay in this room- which is now room 6. (even though this is chapter 4, sorry I built the meditation before I wrote the book)

This also happens to be the meditation doorway behind which my monsters have lived and my psychosis burned out. This is the door behind which we will be visualizing using our attachments, be sick from the hangover or withdrawals, conduct our recovery, and visit to rest in, eventually, in complete peace.

Our attachments relate to us through two beings. They will speak to you as long as you are attached 24 hours a day. Not always in the foreground but they are always there. One is your mental attachment, the other physical. These are demons known as **Hungry Ghosts**.

When googled this is the definition of a hungry ghost:

~Jonathan M. King.~

*According to the Buddha Dharma, there are three main
groups of hungry ghosts: those with no wealth, those with a
little and those with a lot. Those with wealth are broken into
three groups: the torch or flaming mouths, in which food
and drink become flames; the needle mouths, whose throats
are so tiny that food cannot pass through; and the vile
mouths, whose mouths are so decomposed and smelly that
they cannot ingest anything. Among hungry ghosts,
however, most have little or no wealth and are extremely
hungry.*

From now on when you are entering room 6 during
the candle meditation, you will witness yourself on the bed. This
room is dynamic and will alter according to your observations and
requirements during meditations. Upon entering this room, take
time to implement the three objectives of the thought palace into a
mind set. At this moment, it is no longer a room out back to which
we have closed the door in denial, we are living in it! This room
has a leaky ceiling due to the cracked roof tile, the woodwork is
showing through molded wall paper and peeling paint. The rain
and the wind come in here and all color has drained from the room
leaving it in shades of grey. You see yourself huddle under the
blanket feeling like hammered shit. This is where you wake up to
the realization every day that you have an attachment and it's
killing you. Like ground hog day over and over again. Witness this
from the perspective of your mind set and observe your reactions.

And these two **hungry ghosts** with the lousy bedside
manner, let's talk about these two guys for a minute. Both our
ghosts are very real, one is of the world form (physical) the other
is formless (psychological). These demons need a face, know thijn
enemy. If you are going to I-dentify with a concept you may as
well give it a personality, it makes it easier to focus upon as an
external entity. My **physical demon** is Gollum from Tolkien's

66

Lord of the Rings. During my healing days he used to lurk behind the dresser at the end of the bed in room 6, waiting for a moment of weakness to peddle his wares. The physical hungry ghost is the one who talks to you when the withdrawal symptoms set in. Between cigarettes for example, usually after half an hour, the smoker starts to notice urges- *"gotta do something with my hands damn it!"*. Minimal at first but if you leave it another half hour they will start to get short-fused and cranky. The mind gets fuzzy and concentration is awkward. These are the signs that our physical demon is active.

On the other side of the bed is my **psychological demon**; the two dimensional comic strip figure from the MAD comics. His next job is to start to negotiate with the rational mind or sober administrator. Pretty quickly he starts to tell him he has to get out or be held hostage. He can quickly convince us that we need to give in to his demands or we are going to suffer! And he's right, it's the oldest trick in the book. Our society does it to us all the time. It too has its foundations shaky ground. On one hand a corporation feeds us rubbish that makes us sick while another gives us pills that won't make us better, but as long as you keep taking the pills the sickness won't get worse. What a con! Our psychological demon is also selling us a temporary cure to a sickness which is perpetuated through taking the temporary cure!

While you are reading this book and using your attachment, these two guys (or your own two versions of them) will go every where with you, hand in hand. I want you to see them during your meditation in the room with you. They don't have to do much at this point just visualize them as your constant companions, MAD comic figure holding your hand and Gollum sitting on your shoulders with his legs wrapped around your neck. When you start feeling like partaking of your attachment picture Gollum squeezing your neck whispering in your ear

"We wants it precious"

There is a third demon but you'll never get to meet this one although it is a good "revolting concept" to take with you. This third hungry ghost is the one who is with you when you are drunk or stoned out of your mind. A smoker might identify with this demon as active when they have given up giving up and totally embraced the habit, reveling in it. We all know that space, when we've accepted that we are going to die so we may as well enjoy it and smoke ourselves stupid. When we've smoked so much it hurts but we light up another. Or we've gone out and decided to throw all caution to the wind, at a bar or a party. This guy turns up when our psychological MAD demon has taken over from the administrator and is sitting firmly in the driver's seat!

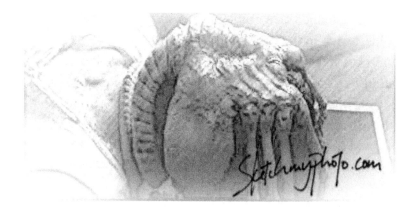

This monster keeps you alive when you no longer remember anything, when you are in bed so comatose that without this guy you even forget to breathe, and some of us still do. This one wants you alive so you can feed him some more misery later. Remember the creature from the film ALIEN? It would burst out of the giant egg shell and with it's hand-like body it would attach itself to the face of the victim causing them to pass out due to suffocation. Its long tail would wrap around the neck and squeeze. Once the victim was out cold it would feed enough nutrients and oxygen to sustain life while it vomited its spawn down into the gut through the digestive tract where the alien fetus would grow. This is our friend when we are *so far away* that we are not even really here anymore. It will nurse us back to health until we are able to take a hair of the dog!

In many ways you carry this demon with you the whole time you are using. A more subtle version but certainly the same demon. As a person using attachments, one becomes not only a different person but you become oblivious to pretty much anything around you which is not involved with getting to use, coming down from, or in the process of using the object of attachment. Attachments rob us of our true identity, our perception of the outside world is flawed and our five senses are focused in the wrong direction. We miss out on the greater reality and the point of living. When this has happened, our attachment has become our destiny and purpose in life, and that is a sad state of affairs.

These few pages have painted a picture of your **thought palace**. It is a *dynamic reality* which will correspond to the dynamics of your attachment as it pulsates its way through this program. Always don the jacket of your three objectives when entering this space.

The pain of cold turkey?

I can speak for attachments to cocaine, nicotine, LSD, alcohol, wrong views and sex. I am not kidding, maybe the coke, I did my best when I was at my most self destructive and still filthy rich but couldn't quite get hooked on it. The mechanism is the same for every addiction. If you stop using the Renunciation method, or Easy Way, you will suffer minimally for three to four days and you might feel a little disorientated for anything up to a week. I quit smoking using the Easy Way method which also doesn't require will power. It was so simple and there was almost no physical pain. I had tried earlier to quit smoking using the will power method and had talked myself into carrying on like a blubbering jack ass. I had convinced myself that I was suffering and in so much pain, poor me what a sacrifice- *all psychological.*

You who have undoubtedly tried to quit will disagree completely at this point, yes I know you went through hell! Been there too. I impressed myself and kept up this second hand existence of abstinence through will power for almost a year. It was better than being a smoker but I reckon the stress of being an abstaining user gave me cancer cells. Not to mention the horror of knowing that I always wanted a cigarette, the horror of looking over my shoulder all the time waiting for the day that I would again be an active smoker. Half of me was in turmoil knowing it would kill me, the other was in turmoil lusting after it all the time but not allowing myself to partake. That is no way to stop. In fact that is not stopping, that's behaving like a vampire who refuses to feed. My point is when I quit using the Easy Way method and the this method, I had to smile at the physical "pain". The physical pain is always played with, used and abused by the psychological hungry ghost or demon who's pain is also way over rated. With Renunciation you see through him, he holds no power any more.

The difference between methods is with will power techniques, the little bastard is screaming for his drug and you are listening, feeling his pain and telling yourself that one day there will be some semblance of solace, while with this method of quitting, you are noticing it but happy that you are about to see the last of him! In this way you are DONE WITH IT! You will *not* become one of those poor bastards who use the AA method wandering around moaning that they are always one drink away from being an alcoholic monster. The point of my slight detour is to explain that their power is only great when you use the will power method. The reason being because using *will* power means you;

stop against your will!

The two demons have no power if you;

stop by choice!

Then you stop because you want to stop, big difference. The "pains" are a reminder that you don't do it anymore, instead of a reminder that you *must not do something* and every time you gently brush them aside they lose their hold on you. They are dying. Each little victory through renunciation is a small moment of enlightenment! With each renunciation, the feelings of attachment grow weaker and the distance between urges lessens, and that is something to smile about! Oh yeah I almost forgot one important tool. There's a nice big baseball bat behind the door in room 6!....

2/ Tools and Weapons.

Right mindfulness is step seven upon the Wheel of Dharma this is for me the most important of the eight steps. Close and deep analysis of this will speedily bring you to the essence of The Middle Way if viewed from the right perspective. Analysis of the four elements mentioned below all working as a whole is crucial to this exercise. The Middle Way is a crucial teaching and will become the basis for your posture during recovery. This chapter will be approached soon, for the time being use this meditation to attempt to understand your perception of your attachments and that I-dentity and association are what makes it all so attractive to you, not the thing itself. The thing you are actually attached to is an *idea* of *yourself* and of your *attachment,* both of which do not exist *anywhere but in your mind.*

This meditation deals with the nature of: *your form-your formless aspect- the true nature of phenomena- your version of it.*

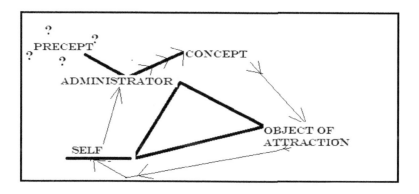

Behind doorway number four in a small box at your feet you will find a scroll:

7 Right Mindfulness-meditation

*Right mindfulness is the controlled and **perfected faculty of cognition.** It is the mental ability to see things as they are, with clear consciousness. The normal thought process is based on judgment, attachment or clinging to old concepts from the past and then an image or concept is formed around an object, person or event. 90% of our perception is formed by these impressions, 10% is actual reality. This happens in the subconscious. Right mindfulness is anchored in clear perception and it penetrates impressions without getting carried away. Right mindfulness allows us to grip the process of <u>conceptualization</u> in a way that actively observes and controls the direction of our thoughts. Buddha explains this with four foundations of mindfulness:*

- *contemplation of the body,*

- *contemplation of the state of mind,*

- *contemplation of the phenomena, and*

- *contemplation of feeling (repulsive, attractive, or neutral)*

*

To achieve a goal of freedom from suffering, access to inner happiness and release from attachments, we are most interested in the balance and understanding between last four points. The following is a breakdown of them.

- **Form** (body): Contemplation of the body relates to the here and now of form on the physical plane. Concentrate on the blood, the bone, the feel of your form. A good technique is to feel with your mind the parts of the body one by one moving up to the top of the head or conversely from the head down. Following the breath in and out is another way to focus on the body paying special attention to the pause between breaths. You might try sounding the ohm as a method of focusing on the form. Acknowledge your physical I-dentity, what it is and how it feels, its potential.

- **Emptiness** (mind): Contemplation of the spaciousness of the mind, the arena of no thought or *chi-spot*. The perspective of the contemplator is of importance here. Understanding of the balance between space and form in that idea's you have create the actions your form carries out. Idea's you have make you sick or well, cause trouble or defuse situations. It is with your mind that you also make attachments and I-dentify with concepts and other forms to create your I-dentity field. It is important to recognize that your formless aspect has one foot in you and the other in the formless world at all times. Be mindful of this segregation, the you with I-dentity and the you without, or the concept you (attached) and the precept you (of the source).

- **Precept** (phenomena): The object across from you, the person at your work with whom you have had a run in. The stock market crash, the event which has caught your attention. For the sake of argument let's say alcohol! Think of the precept as it is, without baggage. If you strip it down to the bare minimum after all the advertising has been removed and the label torn off all you have left is a bottle and some POISON. Granted you think you enjoy its flavor but that is a lie and you know it. You have simply acquired a taste for it just as you did with sugar in your coffee. Even if the wine has been layed down for ten years or stored in oak vats, it is a learned behavior, and just like Tourettes, your compulsive reaction towards your attachment is nothing more than a response to stimulus which ONLY OCCURS WHEN YOU ADD CONCEPTUAL THOUGHT to the equation. Otherwise it is just a bottle of poison which, without conceptualizing it, you would never drink.

- **Concept** (emotion): This is simply what you make of something through your perspective which is put in place by wrong thoughts and bad programming. You hold up your end of the bargain by simply giving value to a thing which holds no intrinsic value what so ever. Similarly, just as you can logically understand the notion of precept- just a bottle of poison, you must see yourself also as what you are without baggage. One unit intimately tied to the universe embracing form, a body- and the formless, a mind. The only directive you have is to help work towards the betterment of humanity, our environment and to face your own karma. If we can leave false perspectives out of the picture we have burned all bridges to attachments. This simply means lose your illusions.

An emotion is our alarm bell. It will let us know that we have work to do so our first reaction to excitement or depression or lust or anger should be self analytical. Start paying attention to your emotions and try to revert to your formless space even if it is only briefly. If you have found your *chi-spot* during meditation you can try to revert to that feeling in your mind. The euphoria of rigpa is a sensation belonging to ultimate truth. Concepts dissolve in the light of ultimate truth. If you have no idea what I mean by ultimate truth that's o.k, we will get to it in detail soon. Let it suffice to say that if we hook up with ultimate truth as perspective, then in a flash illusions (concepts) dissolve through recognition of *their* ultimate truth. Their emptiness of I-dentity comes forward. If you have no idea about ultimate truth, for now attempt to see your vision of the object of your attachment separate from the content. Concentrate on the things that you assume give it value, the advertising hype, the acquired taste and temporary release from suffering which is caused by *IT*. Analise the individual points. Do they bring you any satisfaction individually? Do alcohol advertisements make you happy or thirsty? Why? Where is your acquired taste at 3.30 am when you are groping, desperate for your water? This all comes from *your* concept of IT. You are not attracted to the poison in the bottle or the fag in the box, you are in love with an idea, a learned behavior. Someone who has no attachment to it simply has a different concept of it, or better still, to them it has become a precept. Your I-dentity/

attachment version is an illusion, the truth of it is poison or just rotting vegetable matter and chemicals.

*

Isn't it amazing that we, the most advanced organism ever to roam the planet can be hoodwinked by an idea tossed out into the universe by an advertising company. The dysfunctional parents scenario is a slightly more complicated one but even then, how do we fall for such a trap? Look at the design of us above, the body the mind, the fact that so many wonderful magical things are going on like our ability to create from our imagination, to take an idea from the formless world and make it real, here and now. We can build a pyramid or the empire state building. At the same time we are prone to getting hooked by a simple confidence trick- an idea about I-dentity, not even a good one. It tastes like shit, costs a fortune, will take everything from you and it will kill you. It does absolutely NOTHING for you. Advertising companies must be stunned at how simple it is, like shooting fish in a barrel.

Like it or not, evolution has shown us that as organisms of this world, it is our task to pull down old redundant constructs and rebuild, creating beautiful new forms and concepts built on sturdy wholesome foundations. All things in evolution are moving from chaos towards order, there may be the occasional fall back but this is our inevitable road. Even if we were to fail in this life time, this is our road.

3/ Defects and Antidotes regarding meditation

To manifest speedy changes while on this road, our meditations must become extremely focused which requires tools. The mind is so used to following the hard reality of the five senses that it becomes almost indistinguishable from the world of form with all of its lights, smells and tastes etcetera. Perhaps it is because our understanding of the world of form has been naive up till now through identification with the five senses and grosser self, that our hungry ghost or rogue administrator gets his foot in the door through hi-jacking exciting or dramatic events which which create excitement, fear or depression.(All food for hungry ghosts.) Our goal with the following practice is to find *rigpa* or the natural state of mind *quickly*. To move from the noisy world of form to a space of emptiness in five seconds.

Move as quickly as you can out of your everyday man or woman to a space of no thought in which you are not clinging to any concept nor deflecting dislikes.

1/ You start shutting down the senses. Then

2/ cease all reflections upon sensory experiences, emotions, feelings of happiness and sadness.

3/ Focus the mind on itself in the present moment without allowing it to become preoccupied with memories of the past or plans for the future.

This is the time to descend into rigpa.

*

The purpose of this is to get used to shifting quickly and with ease from any situation into rigpa so that you can access the power of rigpa when you need it. You can make this meditation into a form of Lojong (explained on page 108) by attaching it to a talisman and carrying it with you. This is a very powerful method of suggestion.

For your daily meditations, make this the new starting point for your meditation and do not proceed from this point without achieving rigpa. Out of a space of no thought once you have touched rigpa, allow the mind to commence the candle meditation. If you find it difficult to attain rigpa you have tools. The five defects and the eight antidotes.

The five defects are:

- laziness

- forgetting the object of meditation

- mental dullness and excitement

- not applying the antidote when afflicted by dullness or excitement

- and unnecessary application of the antidotes.

These are the eight antidotes:

- faith

- interest

- perseverance

- pliancy

- mindfulness

- conscientiousness

- application of the antidotes when afflicted by dullness or excitement

- and discarding unnecessary application of the antidotes.

When we say faith it is not referring to the faith so often attributed to religion. This faith means to not hesitate or spend time worrying about not being able to achieve rigpa, hold faith that you will attain your *chi-spot* every time appreciating its benefits. If you cannot quickly descend into rigpa with the accelerated meditation mentioned above you can of course revert to the older method.The point of practicing this "turbo" method is so that you can access it at a moment's need, in busy situations, or when you are put under presure during your transition to becoming a "normal human being". The first four antidotes, faith, interest, perseverance, pliancy counteract laziness, and the fifth antidote, mindfulness, counteracts forgetting the object of meditation. Conscientiousness, the sixth antidote counters dullness and excitement. When the mind is muddy, it must be quickly but gently awakened, breathe deeply in and uplift the mind to start fresh. Excitement should be countered by relaxing the agitated mind, just like a muscle.

Regarding the object or focal point of one's meditation, it is time to use a Buddha image. You can remain with a candle but a statue or picture of the Buddha, perhaps the Dalai Lama or some other Buddhist who is held in high regard. (Preferably one you might be familiar with or have read before). We do this now because you will have started to create an arsenal of qualities and concepts which while they would appear common sense, they are not actually regarded as such within modern society. These things are and have always been aspired towards in Buddhism and an image which is separate from our daily life is a healthy change. You are in the process of change yourself. Think of it as a symbol or mile stone representing that change. Concentrate the mind upon the object when commencing meditation, not allowing it to become distracted by external objects, nor letting it fall into the pits of dullness. The aim is to attain quickly a single pointed concentration joined with sharp clarity. Of course it goes without saying that these antidotes and defects must be memorized and implemented. The entry way to rigpa must become second nature.

Once this is achieved, **special insight** can be added which is covered in the next chapter. The union of calm abiding (single pointed meditation) with special insight (discriminative wisdom) takes us to the arena of manifesting our own destiny.

**The period that follows meditation is of crucial importance. You want to take the essence of meditation with you throughout your day. This post meditation time is where you make this happen. Take the time to contemplate and visualize implementing what you have used in meditation, perhaps attach it to a talisman for Lojong purposes. This is definitely required for things you wish to change in your life like being more compassionate or simply being mindful of compassionate and non-compassionate thoughts.

Apart from step 7- right mindfulness spoken of in Tools and Weapons, your meditation exercises this week consist of implementing the antidotes into your daily routine as well as being mindful of your dynamic Thought Pallace and other concepts presented in chapter 4.

*

Chapter 5

Special Insight and the Nature of Desire

There are those whose minds are bound with various fetters of disturbing emotions like craving desire. Others are in turmoil with different sorts of wrong views. These are all causes of misery; therefore they are always painful, like being on a precipice.

~ Stages of Meditation- HH the Dalai Lama.~

Cultivating Renunciation of Desire -meditation

To understand one's own attachment to desire a good exercise is to observe or bring to mind a person you know who is filled with desire for something or some recognition. The object of desire must be something for which you yourself have no desire whatsoever. Direct your attention toward this desire. Use the memory of a time when your friends desire was on the tipping point of certainty when he or she was not sure if the goal or object would be attained or not, this is when the desire is at its maximum potency. Fill your mind with this recollection while maintaining the utmost inner tranquility. Make the greatest possible effort to be blind and deaf to everything that may be going on around you, and through right concentration a feeling should awaken in your soul. Allow this feeling to rise. This may take many attempts before it works, be patient. Sooner or later you will be able to experience a sensation within, which will correspond to that of the person experiencing the desire and you will notice that while you can experiment with this feeling, you gain a spiritual insight into the soul of the other. This is an excellent method of understanding the language of desire objectively and thus becoming mindful of ones own shortcomings in this department. Never forget to treat the person with whom you are doing this or these exercises with gratitude and reverence. These exercises in no way put you above your fellows.

~Rudolf Steiner-knowledge of higher worlds.~

*

This meditation incorporates special insight and single pointed meditation as spoken of at the end of the last chapter. Observe that you are "multitasking" during this meditation.

A/   in a state of rigpa.
       (chi-spot or no-thought)

B/   Focusing single pointedly upon a friend and his or her conceptualization.
       (allowing a preceptual idea (from your point of view) in while maintaining rigpa, this means to observe the thought objectively)

C/   Investigating and probing the mechanism (of desire) while experiencing the emotions thereof in an objective manner.
       (experiencing and learning about the true nature of desire objectively and without judgment.)

*

Objective observation of someone else's desire, helps us see that desire is the same regardless of the object or concept to which it is tied. Of course you need to choose a form of desire which is about personal gain or self gratification for this exercise, not some desire with an altruistic source. You should not choose a situation in which some one for example desires his wife or attempts to help a sick person recover. These are positive forms of desire and they serve healthy and necessary purposes. Desire in such a situation is tied to love, reproduction, empathy, compassion. Make it a thing which is tied to self gratification.

Suffering desire is not a way of being but a temporary set of circumstances perpetuated generally by choice.

The following is a structure for dealing with suffering and desire in the 3 phases. It is time for you to become acquainted with the nature of the suffering of desire in a clinical way. These are important tools.

*

Dealing with Desire in 3 phases

Desire= craving= suffering= self grasping.

Phase 1:

Our first insight into the true nature of desire is:

*Acceptance of this suffering without making it your own. Recognizing that suffering is the same for everyone and that it is external in nature. We must **not** look at suffering as: "I am afflicted with this suffering and I want it to stop". This sort of concept is identification. If we make it objective, "I am carrying* *this suffering for a while but this too shall pass", it offers us a different perspective with regard to habitual reaction.*

The second insight:

is understanding the <u>origin of suffering</u>. In this way we experience it or go through it in acceptance without running from it or pushing it away with alternative distractions. Better still we allow it to go through us with the knowledge that all things will pass. We must be mindful of the cause and effect of this desire which causes suffering. The primary cause of all our desire and suffering is wrapped up in our illusion of I-dentity, our likes and dislikes, precepts being given their own intrinsic existence through conceptualization and so forth.

The third insight is that it has:

<u>been understood</u>. Suffering in abstinence is nothing more than unlearning a concept. Knowledge of this makes it merely a task which, upon completion, has no hold on you. Like going to the dentist for a tooth ache, you know it'll hurt but then it will fade and eventually there will be no pain. The task is done. It is important to "man-up" to this suffering and make steadfast appointments regarding the commitment to face it, there is <u>no other option</u> which results in the wholesome completion of this suffering. This desire or suffering is brought to an end through recognition of the true nature of the source of it and the fact that understanding this fundamental ignorance is the key to release, otherwise it will stay with us until time slowly transforms suffering into a complex which we will carry further. This then becomes our karma. Recognition that you have no opinion about it means it is done, it has been understood.

It seems easy not to carry out the above mentioned

approach to dealing with desire and it is, in the first stages, but pushing it away or using will power will only bring more suffering in the long run. It leaves little complexes, issues and emotional residue behind, the foot print of unfinished business. Think about this, here is an example of the mind playing tricks on its self so that it gets to keep something it I-dentifies with and take distance at the same time. More commonly known as having your cake and eating it too; You decide to cut down instead of stopping. You know damn well what that means. In the long run you will end up using more, maybe you'll force yourself not to use for a while but that too is suffering and in the end you will get tired of fighting and give in to your desire. Unlearning the mechanism in the way described here in phase 1 is the true and quickest way to be done with it.

We also have a tendency to push suffering away with TV, alcohol, pills, drugs etc. It is partially this black and white way of looking at suffering that perpetuates it. Fight or flight? Acceptance of suffering in whatever form it takes is awakening to the truth of suffering and what lies behind the face of it. Not what our mind makes of it. *We remove blame and identification from suffering.* This way we can tackle the process of purging it.

<u>Phase 2</u>

Negative desire tends to come in three packages.

    1/ the desire for pleasure,
    2/ desire to become and
    3/ the desire to get rid of.

<u>*Kama tanha*</u> *is wanting to experience sensory pleasures. The seeking of things to excite you. Sound familiar?*

<u>*Bhava tanha*</u> *I want to become. The False Self cannot rest in the*

present moment, if it does it gets "found out". It is the nature of the mind to solve problems as a tool. Because the False Self is a rogue concept of the mind which is usually in control, its own survival depends upon solving problems and struggling towards the future. As long as it does this it has a purpose, even when the goal is reached it doesn't take long to find something to be unhappy about or to find something which could be better... It is its nature to express dissatisfaction with the present moment or worse, attachment to the act of not being in the present moment. Wanting to become rich or famous are good examples. Remembering that this pain or desire is nothing more than an alarm bell that <u>you</u> are not present is a good way of flipping this energy or vice.

<u>Vibhava tanha</u> is the desire to get rid of. The identification with getting rid of something like suffering or anger, envy. "When I get rid of this I will be all right". Wanting to get rid of desire is just more of the same and in contradiction with phase 1. The suffering of cold turkey using the will-power method is one of these bizaar conditions.

*

    The trick is not to be busy with the act of identifying with but more reflecting on these idea's. Do not analyze them as *personality traits* that need to be worked on but as elements of something *external* which do not belong and should be done away with. Witness it as such *during meditation from a space of no thought.* When your perspective of dealing with these forms of suffering has moved from contrived to reflex, desire loses much of its momentum. What was once all-encompassing is quickly reduced to;

"Oh yeah that old thing".

Let identifying with it stay with the false Samsaric self and, when it comes knocking, let its presence be a reminder of who you are, or who you are becoming and what is ending. Clinging is part of our paranoia, our insanity. The odd thing is that we tend to cling even harder when we start to recognize that it is the object of our pain which must go. This is a paradox and this is the sign that we are in turmoil, conducting an internal war - schizophrenia.

Desire is never just desire, it brings all of its own baggage with it. It is a beautiful thing to live without desire for something you have conquered, and a wonderful experience to notice it for what it is. The simple antidote to suffering forms of desire is recognition of the form of desire, its working parts and a little time. The old clinging and grasping is akin to the tightening of the grip at your throat by that hungry ghost Gollum who sits on your shoulder responding only to signals of negativity fed to him by the I-dentity. These are the moments, when the grip tightens and you feel it is time to partake in your poison of choice. These are the moments when you would usually hear the hiss in your ear:

We wants it precious!

But what if Gollum were to lean forward and whisper in your ear:

You are responding to conceptual thought stupid!

Either way this is what that base ball bat behind the door in room 6 is for. Start visualizing your self throwing your hungry ghost from your shoulders and beating him black and blue. Hear the cracking bone and visualize the blood spatters. Negative emotions brought about by ingesting poisons are outward expressions of internal psychotic episodes experienced by a Schizophrenic. Never focus on the object of desire unless as a precept, that is attachment and identification, _concentrate on the desire itself_, then you will laugh.

Practice this throughout your day with little things so you can experience the techniques of letting go. Letting go is a moment of enlightenment, holding on is just the mind playing games.

"It is only when we believe things to be permanent that we shut off the possibility of learning from change. If we shut off this possibility, we become closed, and we become grasping. Grasping is the source of all of our problems. Since impermanence to us spells anguish, we grasp on to things desperately, even though all things change. We are terrified of letting go, terrified, in fact, of living at all, since learning to live is learning to let go. And this is the tragedy and the irony of our struggle to hold on: not only is it impossible, but it brings us the very pain we are seeking to avoid."

~Sogyal Rinpoche-The Tibetan Book of Living and Dying~.

The more often you let go the weaker the clinging becomes. Remember the goblin on your shoulder with his fingers around your neck. When clinging to desire arises, club him half way to death, his grip weakens more every time. Even a Buddhist can take pleasure in this violence. Be grateful for the red flags, they remind you that you are not conscious. Understanding that you are free of desire comes when you notice that you _no longer have any opinion or judgments about it._

Phase 3

The mind will experience these insights only through contemplation and reflection and the Eureka moment comes as awareness. Awareness cannot be explained and words can only indicate a direction to look in. It is only in this state of mind that the end of suffering *is already* achieved and that non-attachment to suffering or desire is realized. Phase 3 involves the relationship between our selves, our attachment and the impermanent, constantly changing nature of both of them.

Through our ignorance we attach to sensory (temporary) pleasures to distract ourselves from our own dissatisfaction with the way we live our lives. We have all heard before that drug abuse is a form of escapism, this is true but from what? Escapism is a form of pushing things away that we (our I-dentity with all its baggage) have decided we don't want to acknowledge or deal with. Perhaps we don't realize it or admit it, but the ultimate thing that we desperately do not want to face up to is our own demise. That would signify the end of all liking and disliking, clinging and deflecting. Such an attachment to death *is* suffering. Using attachment as a distraction from the business of living and dying is a form of throwing away our lives because we don't want to throw away our lives! All things that we experience with our senses are temporary so when we identify with pleasures of the senses we are indirectly identifying with death or impermanence, desperately trying to cling to some elusive moment, something....better, something permanent. Ironically, our identification with these little deaths is an attempt to distract us from our own mortality or the idea that we should be doing something better with our preciouse time, which is only a reminder we are going to die. We then behave as the quintessential Japanese tourist, taking photo's and crossing off tourist sights on our list before rushing of to the next Eiffel Tower to do the same. Of course because we are so busy with the idea of getting it all on film, we forget to experience the real thing which means we are left with a bunch of photo's we could have seen in any magazine. Samsaric selves are always trying to improve the quality of their lives by getting more things or experiencing bigger sensory pleasures. Even the dwindling of the *effect* of our attachment from the moment of inset is symbolic of this impermanence.

This repetitive and mistaken way of living is comparable to the very nature of drug attachment and contaminated happiness. It is this aspect which brings about the onset of the suffering of change. These short lived distractions die in pain quite quickly but because you use it to distract yourself from reality you will do it again but the cycle will shorten and the amount will increase and in no time we're all Japanese again. Using crutches, being sold under the guise of pleasurable distractions, to a false self trying desperately to push away reality so it won't have to face its own impermanence, is living in fear. This is why I call the horror, the 3.30 am wake up sweats- *"the Fear"*.

An understanding of these three phases allows us to see desire and suffering for what they are, to understand them and to let them go as understood. Through contemplation and not through self persecution or judgment, we can comfortably let go of the things in us which we "desire" or for which we are suffering in full free will. Free will or will power, which is literally *Vibhava tanha*... Through repeating this contemplation we can come to let go instead of striving to evolve into some one better or chastising ourselves, which are again both forms of desire. This is the reason the will power method is little more than a form of prolonged torture with a 5% success rate. Nirvana is reached not through the struggle to attain but through release in awareness. The message is we are already there, we have already arrived, the only thing in the way is perception.

Because this is an exercise in confronting elements of yourself which you have spent a lifetime trying to subdue, it may appear to get worse before it gets better, but in recognizing the experience for what it is, you recognize the recovery process as you are in it and this can even make it pleasurable. If you think something is too big for you, you are again in the mind which is always doing the math and busy with the future, come back to now- deal with this moment. Despair, agitation, aggression may flair up but don't forget to allow yourself to suffer, this only means you are going through to cessation of suffering. In doing this we must come to know that these desires and sufferings are not ours personally and they are not ours to hold onto. Just let go. Suffer properly, make it count. That is a gaining of merit.

*

The purpose of the next few paragraphs will be to cultivate an understanding of **Special Insight.** Our goal will be as follows;

Move quickly to rigpa and from there we will attain special insight whilst maintaining a state of rigpa. Through special insight we come to understand what is meant by the Buddhist term ultimate truth,we begin to touch upon the true nature of reality-emptiness.

The Buddhist concept of emptiness refers to a lack of I-dentity or self in all things including us. This is what is meant in the Wheel of Dharma step 7 Right Mindfulness with the line *"see things as they truly are, to see their true nature."* I had trouble trying to grip this oneness concept or lack of identity. It almost seems like you are being robbed and I guess we are in a strangely liberating fashion. Try this metaphor for dummies as an explanation.

Special Insight Contemplation.

Imagine you have a bright light bulb and a black sheet of cardboard. The black sheet represents the boundaries of our dimension. Hold the cardboard up so that it blocks the light. The sheet is full of tiny pin holes which allow little beams of light to shine through. The light is the source or essence of life, unending and represents the world of the formless. On one side of the cardboard the light is ubiquitous, on the other, just tiny little defiant beams of light shooting out into the darkness until they falter and run out.

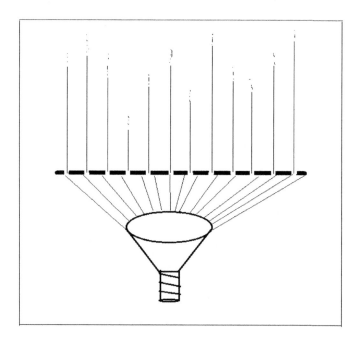

Here and now on this plane we are the beams of light and though it would seem that we are individuals with an identity and a reality, the truth of the matter is that we are all joined at the hip so to speak. Bigger hole or smaller one, the light

that shines through is the same stuff. If you consider that your body is made out of fresh water (70%) and star dust (the rest), then by definition your form has been and will be re-used time and again. Couple this with the knowledge that the world of form and the world of the formless waste nothing, then death becomes really an abstract concept. *Couple this with the knowledge that your I-dentity is just a concept, an idea in your head, then you can only come to one conclusion.

You don't actually exist but at the same time,

you are all there is.

Remember Steiners discussion (page 35) regarding the body before and after death? Seen as such, the mind dies, the body dies, the essence or *life force simply retreats* from the world of form as it is understood on this side of the cardboard sheet and then the natural path of decay sets in, essence of self has left the building. Understanding this entails receiving glimpses of your self *without* self or I-dentity. The sudden shock that you don't exist can be heavy for many people. On one hand you lose your entire sense of self or I-dentity and on the other you become immortal and gain a sense of absolute belonging. Everything means something else, even idea's, it is literally quite a sobering concept in that realizing it or glimpsing it puts all things in perspective suddenly including the illusion of our attachments.

Another viewpoint which I found helpful when trying to get my head around this concept of- "phenomena having no intrinsic self" was to be found in a discussion or interview I followed with a spiritualist physicist by the name of Tom Campbell (author of *My Big Toe*) He questioned:

When a tree falls in the forest if there is no sentient being present, does it make a sound?

The answer is of course no. Why is this difficult to grasp? Because we give the crashing, thundering cacophony of a tree falling in the forest to the object as a fundamental part of its make up. Sure, you can picture the entire scene, it wouldn't be of this world if it *was not* so, the tree is heavy, it falls, dumb question! The truth of the matter is that the noise is for our benefit and it registers *to* us *inside our head!* You need eardrums to decipher the waves traveling through the air as "noise" other wise you wouldn't even be aware of it until it hit you on the head. The illusion is, we associate it with the tree, but the reality is, *the noise belongs to us!* Our senses are constantly tricking our mind into figuring reality. Because we see ourselves in this peculiar way of separation and self gratification, we project our concept of reality onto everything we see, taste, hear, smell and feel thus giving other phenomena its own intrinsic I-dentity or self, this is me, that is you. I am here, you are over there. This me and you is merely life popping up to put its head above ground just as those light beams are the same light that shines behind the cardboard sheet.

No conditioned phenomena has an intrinsic self!

Our sensory perspirations are a little like Newtonian physics, they're great, but just for the really big stuff. If there were an intrinsic self, don't you think science or would have found it by now? They can't. They are still missing the driver and the power source! Oddly we fail to find this astounding. In everything that exists we dig out its power source to find out how it works, if we need power we dig rotting forests out of the ground to get at it in the form of oil. We even have good old Newtonian physics giving us laws of science like:

You cannot get more energy out of a thing than you put into it.

When we look towards our own power source, it is suddenly a miracle or some such thing. The mind, our driver, the seat of the self is nowhere to be found! The objects we refer to, such as the tree, is given its I-dentity by us through our senses, just as our drug of choice. But as we have seen our senses feed us a distorted version of reality through our mis-perception of them. We have come to a clincher from which we can not logically work our way out. This forces us to recognize that our perception, when utilized from a Samsaric or ignorant point of view, is radically out of sync with true reality. We conceptualize, giving objects their own intrinsic self.

Recognizing the absence of intrinsic self within an object is to recognize its EMPTINESS but at the same time its absolute connectedness to everything else, and that is the origin of the power source, and the driver.

This new information is easy to forget when your throwing darts with a mate in the local pub and drinking beer but it is enough at this time to have these glimpses. The good thing about receiving glimpses of ultimate reality or truth, is you can not un-see it. There is no way back and that in itself means if you were to stop reading this book now, you would still quit your attachment or be driven back to stopping because you have had a taste of the answer to the ultimate question!

Meditation, like good music or art, manages to sneak in behind the ego delivering its message to the heart. Special insight allows us to discriminate correctly ensuring us that the message has its foundations on solid ground. In the act of doing this, two things are happening at once.

1/ Achieving rigpa (the message of emptiness is being delivered) and

2/ recognizing the <u>identity of self and phenomena as illusion</u>. More important than recognizing identity as illusion is holding onto the mechanism behind the knowledge.

*This mechanism is akin to the way we allow great music and art to sneak in or by-pass ego-regulatory systems. This understanding can create an intense space of freedom and spaciousness while embedding great wisdom. The wisdom of the nature of all things. This is ultimate truth, the understanding of **special insight** (perspective offered by the knowledge of I-dentity in relation to attachments, the lack of intrinsic self) in combination with a certain discriminative wisdom, namely the perspective of all life as one equal entity. To recognize the common spark in all things (more about this later). Once you are reasoning with ultimate truth you have no illusions and therefore you can only make correct decisions.*

<u>You contemplate with the reality that is behind concept!</u>

From this perspective and while meditating, special insight, wisdom of the selflessness of phenomena, understanding of precepts and concepts, allows us to direct our thoughts with a different kind of vision. Once tasted, one is obliged to go forwards. It could be described as being as honest with yourself as you ever have been, are, or ever will be, and that is a healthy space from which to consider our predicament.

At this point it should be made clear that hanging onto one space more than the other can cause problems. The two must marry for further development. Special insight tends to be born of an intelectual earth and descriminative wisdom is the more left brain sort of cognitive activity. The meditations behind door number 5 are; Cultivating renunciation of desire, Right intention and Positivity exercise.

2 Right intention- meditation from the wheel of dharma

*Right intention refers to the mechanical aspect of wisdom and, right intention addresses the forward push of our understanding. This is all about **commitment to ethical and mental self-improvement.** Buddha describes three types of right intention:*

- *Denial of desire.*

- *Resistance to volatile negative emotion. (it has no place in reality)*

- *The intention of <u>harmlessness,</u> : do not think or act out of aggression, develop compassion.*

  - *This encompasses a diligence of the mind and a purity of body and spirit. It involves correct thought and concentration, allowing only constructive thought which, if carried out correctly, removes junk from the mind without effort. This is about renunciation of the ego.*

~Wheel of Darmha~

*

Positivity -exercise

Search for the beauty in life even in unattractive situations. Do not dwell on the negative and maintain a mindfulness of dark idea's and impulses as they arise. Be wary of cynicism and negative impulse reflex reaction. When they arise, counter them with love. Search for a ground or space to which you can return when these feelings are noticed.

~R. Steiner- 6 Complementary Exercises.~

*

Chapter 6

Bodhichitta & Bodhisattva

*The awakening mind of **Bodhichitta**, is the mind that begins
to realize the <u>why</u> of striving toward awakening of
compassion for the benefit of all sentient beings.
Understanding why brings motivation and motivation means
the compassion you feel is yours, not a forced thing. It is
real.*

When we become accustomed to special insight through
meditation, the way we look at our fellow humans also changes.
Imagine a conflict from the past in which you both thought you
were correct and allowed it to escalate. Armed with the knowledge
of special insight and discriminative wisdom, you would probably
react differently now. It is the knowledge of our common bond, not
only in our wish for peace and happiness but also our very essence
unfettered by ego and or I-dentity, which softens us towards our
fellow humans. Suddenly we are experiencing a difference of
opinion held by the guy in the mirror instead of our sworn enemy
or the guy you can't stand at work. In fact, from this new
perspective, to suggest that you can't stand someone no longer
makes any sense, it implies objectivity in a subjective situation.
The minute you have started to "not be able to stand" somebody
you are no longer looking out from the correct perspective, the ego

or I-dentity has re-entered the game offering separation issues and conceptual thought. Bodhichitta must move from contrived thought to reflex, otherwise there is always room for the ego to step in and make a mess. Hopefully by now the way we look at our attachment has also changed radically. Once again, during our preparation for combat with our attachments, we will always notice flashes and old patterns until the new knowledge and understanding become reflex.

Programing the mind to be rid of these afflictions in the quickest possible way is achieved through meditation. Firstly waking up to the fact that we have been operating out of misinformation from birth forwards, and secondly reprogramming the mind with healthy, solid foundations. When the penny drops the truth of our misconceptions and disillusionment as a species is shocking which only helps to drive us on. The path of the Bodhisattva begins with understanding the awakening mind of Bodhichitta.

Why do I need to know this?

- Because it allows you guide lines which enable decisive growth and limits your incoming stress levels.

- It allows you to step into the loop of generating positivity.

- It allows you to move your attention away from your attachment and be busy with its demise at the same time.

Bodhichitta comes in two types, **conventional** and **ultimate**. Conventional bodhichitta involves the cultivation of the initial thought that aspires to attain perfectly consummated Buddha-hood in order to benefit all sentient beings. This is achieved by cultivating Bodhichitta as a **contrived experience**

through forced or steered acts of compassion combined with the previously mentioned meditations relating to compassion. This is the state of the *awakening* mind of Bodhichitta. In combination with deeper knowledge of The Middle Way this becomes ultimate Bodhichitta. When this state is attained the experience has become reflex through your practise and your understanding of the reasoning behind a compassionate posture. It has matured.

The fundamental teaching of Buddha is that we should view others as being more important than we are. Of course you can not completely ignore yourself, but neither can you neglect the welfare of other people and other sentient beings, particularly when there is a clash of interests between your own welfare and the welfare of other people. At such a time you should consider other peoples welfare more important than your own personal well being. Compare yourself to the rest of humanity. They are many while you are just one person. Your suffering and happiness may be important, but it is the experience of just one individual, whereas the happiness of all other sentient beings is immeasurable and countless. Spok hit the nail on the head in the film "Wrath of Kahn" when he said

"Logic clearly dictates that the needs of the many outweigh the needs of the few."

So it is the way of the wise to sacrifice one or few for the benefit of the majority and it is the way of the foolish to sacrifice the majority on behalf of just one single individual. Remember the meditation regarding the egotistical version of yourself with all the bread? This is why our greed based society is bound to collapse, the wrong guy gets the bread and holds onto it until it goes moldy. Your attachment belongs to that world. Even from the point of view of your personal well being, you must cultivate a compassionate mind. This is the source of true happiness in life and a lack of it is one of the main reasons for the unpleasant, relentless hum and boredom of an unfulfilling reality. This is the road less traveled as opposed to the quick fix of a form based, materialistic outlook.

It is in the nature of evolution for life to go forwards weather it be a bunch of cells in a Petri dish or a village of human beings. *Everything* in the universe *wants* to move from chaos towards order. It is literally in our DNA. Compassion, co-operation and kindness, these things are intimately connected with evolution and order. Things like cancer are anomalies, mutated generally by man through pollution, attachments, too much sugar or genetic modification. Cancer, being born out of junk and on unsteady foundations will behave against nature, attacking the host until it dies, killing itself in the process. I don't believe that humans are inherently corrupt, I can't look upon the human race as a cancer although it appears to be behaving as one, destroying the earth and not caring for one another. Our progress is not progress if we live in inequality and destroy the planet killing the host.

The above is a pretty fair description of cancer, and while we display these traits, they are not inherent in humans. The cancer of humanity is the corruption which *is* the lack of equality, and that, just like the programming which brought us our strange perspective with regard to attachments, causes all the trouble. That is the cancer, and that is why Bodhichitta is needed now more than ever. It is the antidote to a lack of equality! It is also an antidote to the self serving nature of attachments and all of their paranoia and schizophrenia.

If you think about the cancer that is a lack of equality compared to the wholesome co-operation suggested in the fundamental teachings of the Buddha, you can draw parallels to your attachment and the way you deal with it in your daily life. Your internal struggle always ends up with the right intentions caving into the will of the drug (which of course has no will of its own). It's very similar to our propensity for corruption in what is supposed to be an otherwise free and democratic society. The deal is offered but we tend to lean towards inequality every time. We do this on a psychological level and on a physical level. You have negative emotions and use your attachment. This gives you a false sense of release (contaminated happiness), a crutch, whatever, it is still a lie and your repeated consent only takes you further down the road towards more corruption and negative emotion, further away from the wholesome way of ultimate truth. This is psychologically damaging, perpetuating the cyclic existence and cyclic negative energy of Samsara, feeding a depressive self image which will make choices accordingly. This unwholesome habit or subconsciously repeated tick/ spasm brought about by negative emotion is represntative of that same cancer, and this sick posture opens the mental doorway allowing easier access for your demons to get a foothold while on a physical level, well, I know I don't need to tell you anything about that. Once again, we choose the bad stuff over the wholesome.

Think back to the analogy of one being as opposed to the needs of the many. Imagine these beings as a collective which makes up you the individual. Which part of you is this psychological "one single individual" for whom the rest of you (the majority of common sense) must be sacrificed, who doesn't care what anybody else thinks, does or says;

"whatever, I am going to smoke that joint and sniff that coke anyway!"

This is the version or aspect of you who uses when they know they really shouldn't, or the smoker who looks over towards the passenger seat where his child is sitting as he/ she considers lighting up. Or when the whole family and some of your *real* friends are starting to show concern. Do you brush their concerns aside feeling attacked? Where is compassion now? Where is your recognition of compassion from another towards yourself?

"It's my life, I'm fine, leave me alone, mind your own business"!

Or, does it touch you that they are concerned? You understand yourself that you really are doing something stupid but can't stop. The way you respond to those who care about you can tell you a lot about your mental posture in relation to your attachment as well as compassion. A compassionate outlook helps greatly for one who is about to quit, in the middle of going cold turkey, or in the grip of an attachment problem. It can help you relate better to those who care about you but it can also help you quit. It is a move toward ultimate truth, not away from it. Compassion is in the same corner as ultimate truth, and you need both of them in your corner!

The awakening mind of Bodhichitta must be contrived until it becomes spontaneous action as stated. You will have quit your attachments long before this happens but if you wish to take Buddhism seriously, ultimate Boddhichitta (reflex) must be learned before you move on to become a true Bodhisattva.

Patrul Rinpoche (Tibetan master) explains the three degrees of Bodhichitta as such:

1/ The way of the king who seeks only to increase his wealth and power but comes to realize that his own prosperity and good fortune depends on the that of his subjects.

2/ The way of the ferry man who takes his passengers across the water and in the act of doing so ferries himself as well.

3/ The way of the shepherd, who takes care of the welfare of his herd placing their safety and wellbeing above that of himself.

*

Tonglen is a well known and simple meditation practice which you can practice anywhere, anytime. Its purpose is to:

- Strengthen your sense of renunciation

- Reduce selfish attachment

- Create merit generating positive karma

- Developing and expanding Bodhichitta

While it is a simple and handy ready to go meditation, it encompasses all of the **Six Perfections**;

giving, ethics, patience, joyous effort, concentration and wisdom. These are the practices of a Bodhisattva.

In the meditation, one visualizes taking onto oneself the suffering and pain of others on the in-breath, and on the out-breath giving peace, happiness and success to all sentient beings.

*

If you are about to quit or just experimenting with periods of abstinence it is a handy technique to take with you in your daily life. You may also adjust this to fit your own attachment. For example breathing in all the suffering experienced during denial of desire and breathing out all the positive things you wish to achieve after you've quit including your peace of mind. When you feel an urge focus on this meditation. You can even do this in a traffic jam. Then break down what the truth is of the desire and suffering, not the romanticized version that your ego drags around all day long. Any suffering you are experiencing you can put to good use by administering the practice of tonglen. Imagine your suffering to be the suffering of all sentient beings as you breathe in. Indeed your cure (and so your suffering) will eventually benefit and guide others not to mention the solace and concern of your loved ones. Imagine how proud they will be of you when you finally cast your ball and chain aside. With your out-breath this can represent the giving of peace, happiness and success to all beings. Imagine how proud you will feel yourself! The Dalai Lama is said to practice tonglen daily and has stated the following about this practice;

"Whether it helps others or not I gain peace of mind through it, then I can be more effective, and that benefit is immense."

Lojong is another mind training Dzogchen technique. It is based on affirming through aphorisms and its goal is to refine and purify ones perspective and state of mind. Lojong is broad consisting of fifty nine slogans designed to offer antidotes to undesired states of mind and adjusting many viewpoints. This is not for us here and now, your purpose is simply to quit and so you will custom design your practice of lojong. Once again, this is a technique for the quitter on the move. We implement these slogans and affirmations to act as little *Lojong Guardians* who stand watch at the gate way of your synapses.

Reflex responses to stimulus is all that is happening when you are triggered towards attachment. One of the main reasons that it's "difficult" to quit attachments is that your brain gets used to automating stuff. This results in the brain building big fat synaptic highways into your response system or automated neurological transmissions. Lojong offers you a little mind ninja who can act as an antidote. Notice the event and your reaction. Stop and take time to recognize and acknowledge this. Implement your affirmation and recognize the actual biological aspect of the situation regarding synapses. Visualize the breaking of ties fed to you by your psychological demon, the construction worker in your brain who loves to build these little mischievous bridges of automation. We are cutting the desire synapse down in its tracks, implementing lojong and building new bridges. You will use it to couple commitments and perspectives experienced during meditation into your routine but also to implement during crisis moments. These affirmations are yours to build and implement, here are a couple of examples which I used;

The permanent suffering of remaining in abuse is much worse than the temporary suffering of quitting abuse. Letting go is a moment of enlightenment, holding on is just mind games.

*

Suffering experienced when one has truly decided to quit represents the passing of permanent sufferings.

I know how to deal with suffering.

*

The only guide line required is that you build in recognition of your new perspective. Remind yourself of the truth with a short to the point sentence or two that are easy to remember, nothing long winded. The idea is to give you easy access tunnel vision when you need it. Kind of like putting trainer wheels on your child's bike so he or she can get use to riding without the danger of falling. Use this technique to start reducing your intake or restraining yourself at certain times, get use to the feeling.

*

What is a **Bodhisattva**? When googled, you will come up with things like;

The term Bodhisattva was used by the Buddha in reference to himself in his previous lives and as a young man in his (then current) life when he attained Buddha hood, prior to his enlightenment, as he was working towards his own liberation. Upon recounting his experiences as a young aspirant, he regularly used the phrase "When I was an unenlightened Bodhisattva etc" The term therefore refers to one who is "bound for enlightenment". In other words, a person whose aim is to become fully enlightened. In the Pāli canon, the Bodhisattva is also described as one who is still subject to birth, illness, death, sorrow, defilement, and delusion.

For our purposes this means one who has awakened to the fact that they are going to quit and has understood and is agreement with all the principals discussed in this book up till now. No this doesn't mean we have a secret Bodhisattva club, it means you have committed to the fact that *it* **is going to happen!** It is not time to panic, but it is time to be resolute and by the way, the panic **will not come.** The feelings of panic and

"Oh I don't know it probably won't work for me, I am different than everybody else."

or

"I am still not ready, maybe I can't do this!"

those feelings are at their worst *right now!* By the time you have reached the end of this book, you will be like a dog choking himself on his leash in desperation to get at it! Once the commitment has been made and the facts understood, there is only elation and the matter of choosing the date. Perhaps you feel as if you are really not ready to quit or get committed, fear not, by the end of the book you will be fine and anyway we are not there yet. If there is any doubt or you are still thinking things like;

> *"But I drink to have fun, there won't be any fun in my life if I can't socialize."*

then it's time to re-read. Poisoning yourself is;

A)   not fun and

B)   not at all a social activity.

       Skim reading this book doesn't work and any question to this effect means;

A/   Important information has not been realized. If you have understood the text but still have these questions then meditate upon what you know.

B/   You may be simply extremely nervouse about your ability to deal with your little old attachment. If it's a case of proper diligence whith meditation and proper understanding of the teaching then it is just nervs and that's o.k.

       By now you should be able to counter any argument in favor of your attachment with arguments built on solid ground, common sense and logic. FYI, you will have more fun as a non-user than as a user any day!

       As a Bodhisattva, your abstinence and if you like your enlightenment, are achieved through clearing out the negative emotions of the mind. To do this we have tools, meditation and wisdom or practice and theory. The antidotes and information gathered up till now are what we have to counter these negative emotions but there is further instruction which sets it all in stone. It is time to cultivate the philosophical view known as the Middle Way, or Madhyamika. This is dealt with in the next chapter. For the time being, this chapters purpose is to introduce you to the practice of tonglen and lojong for use when the moment presents itself, and of course compassion toward your self and your fellow humans.

Openness of ones mind and heart

Approach all new events from a space of new thought, without prejudice and with a clear mind. Be wary of programming and do not allow programming to obscure the truth of new experiences in your life.

~R. Steiner- 6 Complementary Exercises.~

*

Chapter 7

The Middle Way

*To become a Buddha one must cultivate virtues,
including loving kindness, but they are no
substitute for wisdom knowing emptiness because
they do not counteract the perspective of grasping
at the self. Direct knowledge of emptiness is the
only antidote powerful enough to eliminate the
root of cyclic existence.*

~HH the Dalai Lama- From Here to Enlightenment~

*

The surface understanding of the Middle Way is
to avoid extreme highs and lows, excessive activity and too
much inactivity. To find a middle way between the peeks and
valleys. Through following this road, in combination with the
teachings, the deeper meaning of the Middle Way becomes
apparent to us. This is the recognition of these dualistic
phenomenon from a space or perspective *beyond their grasp.*

While contemplating the following sutra, be mindful of
the common condition of the two polarities. Ignorance! The
sutra suggests to escape ignorance is, in principle, to escape
Samsara, cyclic existence. It suggests we live among the
trappings of Samsara whilst being mindful of the psychosis

of this ignorance and the duality it creates. This same principle can be put to excellent use when applied to your own situation in relation to your attachment.

The Middle Way school posits a "middle way" position between metaphysical claims that things ultimately either exist or do not exist. Nagarjuna's influential Verses on the Middle Way deconstructs the usage of terms describing reality, leading to the insight into emptiness. it contains one reference to a sutta by the Buddha himself, namely the Samyutta Nikaya's Kaccāyanagotta Sutta:

the Samyutta Nikaya's Kaccāyanagotta Sutta:

Kaccayana Gotta approached the Blessed One and, on arrival, having bowed down, sat to one side. As he was sitting there he said to the Blessed One: "Lord, 'Right view, right view,' it is said. To what extent is there right view?"

"By & large, Kaccayana, this world is supported by a polarity, that of existence & non-existence. But when one sees the origination of the world as it actually is with right discernment, 'non-existence' with reference to the world does not occur to one. When one sees the cessation of the world as it actually is with right discernment, 'existence' with reference to the world does not occur to one.

"By & large, Kaccayana, this world is in bondage to attachments, clinging s (sustenances), & biases. But one such as this does not get involved with or cling to these attachments, clingings, fixations of awareness, biases, or obsessions; nor is he resolved on 'my self.' He has no uncertainty or doubt that just stress, when arising, is arising; stress, when passing away, is passing away. In this, his knowledge is independent of others. It's to this extent, Kaccayana, that there is right view.

"'Everything exists': That is one extreme. 'Everything doesn't exist': That is a second extreme. Avoiding these two extremes, the Tathagata teaches the Dhamma via the middle:

116

From ignorance as a requisite condition come fabrications. From fabrications as a requisite condition comes consciousness. From consciousness as a requisite condition comes name-&-form. From name-&-form as a requisite condition come the six sense media. From the six sense media as a requisite condition comes contact. From contact as a requisite condition comes feeling. From feeling as a requisite condition comes craving. From craving as a requisite condition comes clinging/sustenance. From clinging/sustenance as a requisite condition comes becoming. From becoming as a requisite condition comes birth. From birth as a requisite condition, then aging & death, sorrow, lamentation, pain, distress, & despair come into play. Such is the origination of this entire mass of stress & suffering.

"Now from the remainderless fading & cessation of that very ignorance comes the cessation of fabrications. From the cessation of fabrications comes the cessation of consciousness. From the cessation of consciousness comes the cessation of name-&-form. From the cessation of name-&-form comes the cessation of the six sense media. From the cessation of the six sense media comes the cessation of contact. From the cessation of contact comes the cessation of feeling. From the cessation of feeling comes the cessation of craving. From the cessation of craving comes the cessation of clinging/sustenance. From the cessation of clinging/sustenance comes the cessation of becoming. From the cessation of becoming comes the cessation of birth. From the cessation of birth, then aging & death, sorrow, lamentation, pain, distress, & despair all cease. Such is the cessation of this entire mass of stress & suffering."

*

The sequence of events mentioned above refers to the "twelve links". There is an excellent study of this in the book "The Middle Way" by HH the Dalai Lama for any who would choose to delve into this.

To approach practicing the Middle Way, we must prepare our lives a bit. This means defining what is important to us and minimizing our stuff so that we can put our attention where it needs to be with the necessary force and clarity. Clearing away nonsense and frivolous, time wasting activities is an important aspect of the apprentice Bodhisattva's way of life. This does not mean that you are limited to meditation and lentils for the rest of your life although monastic practices can be very rewarding and there is nothing wrong with a lentil or two! It means that for the period between now and the time you have realized that you no longer have any opinion about your soon to be X-attachment, you will limit your focus to what is important in your life, reduce unnecessary stress levels and external stimulus. See it as a breaking down of data, so that your daily activities are not too much and that you can give them your full attention completing each task to the best of your ability. Avoid too much excitement but stay busy with relevant phenomena and events.

The practical aspect discussed here explains the Middle Way as realized by the Buddha after he had experienced asceticism (the denial of almost all sustenance as a form of seeking enlightenment), and after the opposite, absolute debauchery and excess while hunting for happiness. This scenario is depicted in the Herman Hesse novel Siddhartha which portraits a way of living between extremes to create a happier existence.

A short detour.

**   It is important to realize that you are not simply quitting your attachment in a time of no stress and that when more stress does enter your life, you will be able to handle it without reaching for the good old stress crutch again. The removal of the illusion of "crutch" is the admition that there never was a broken leg in the first place. In fact you will be better equipped to handle stress than ever before, the question is will you want to? Unnecessary stress should generally be avoided although unavoidable problems come. Usually someone with a working knowledge of Buddhist principals will relish these opportunities to exercise their wisdom and or learn. Further more, what we consider to be stressful problems while in the throws of negative attachment are usually just events in daily life for normal folk. Something to be dealt with and forgotten about.

** If you have lost your job due to your attachment I am truly sorry. I have lost much and destroyed much through attachments, so I *do* understand. Many people hit rock bottom losing everything before they face up to the fact that their attachment is to blame. No one can give you anything back which you may have lost or destroyed but I can promise you that if you finish this book, practice and understand the instructions and teachings that you will be free of your attachments as am I. From that moment forwards you will start to build your life up instead of break it down. This is the same for drinkers and smokers as it is for heroin users or those suffering a bad relationship.

We are going to create a **mood board/shrine**. Choosing what to jettison and what to keep can be tricky but there are guidelines which may help. Some stuff you simply can't get rid of, like work. Hopefully you have a job you like, maybe you don't and maybe you lost it. It is something which takes up much of your time and the way you approach time consuming things in your life has an impact on your quality of life, so, if you have one, it is one of the things to take with you in your stuff pile. Other things which take up your time and are important to you may be things like family, time with your children, a hobby, something creative like playing an instrument, church, fitness. There may be something you aspire towards like moving to a new house in the near future.

Out of all the stuff in your life work out what plays a part and what you would like to put aside and not spend time on for a while, or permanently. For example, my current shrine/ mood board has representations of the following.

- I am working on this book.

- Planning to build an environmentally friendly, off grid cottage for myself and my partner.

- My work, which represents saving money to build the cottage and providing an income, as well as exercises in compassion (I work with young people who have suffered abuse) and of course.

- My meditation practices, their further development and mine as an apprentice Bodhisattva.

These four things are presently my main focus. (I exercise daily but that is a given and for me is like sleeping or breathing so I don't count it. Also my partner is the most important person in my life but that is a permanent aspect of my life, a bit like my right arm, this mood board is for daily activities outside of right arms). The next step is to take a symbol or representation of these things and place them in the vicinity of your focus point or meditation space.

I have

- A copy of my first book which I bound by hand, this is a representation of my work on this book.

- A book about how to build an eco friendly house.

- A portrait of myself drawn by one of my clients. This represents my work.

- A copy of the the Perfection of Wisdom and the Avatamsaka Sutra (practices and vows of the Bodhisattva Samanthadra).

When you are about to settle into meditation take a few minutes to mentally review these things, cement their importance, monitor their progress then let it go and commence meditation. During moments when you are experimenting with abstinence and urges you can also revert to these as far more important things to focus attention on than day dreaming about inhaling rotting combusted vegetable matter into your lungs or drinking it. Also in times of stress or uncertainty, revert to your mood board and ask yourself- Is this relevant to my practice at the present moment. If not drop it.

By minimizing focus and activities while paying attention to the spaces in between, you start to relax into life and give yourself time to breathe. This should be practiced daily by everyone on the planet but alas to pinch a line; *"the world is too much with us"*, (or we allow ourselves to get sucked into it). Just as in meditation, focus on each element with your full power and then when you are done, *let it go.*

Madhyamika

I can't say it enough so I'll say it again as it is of crucial importance before continuing. A steadfast ability is required so that one can operate on two levels at the same time. Calm abiding and special insight or special insight combined with descriminative wisdom. This means single pointed concentration during meditation and the ability to activate other teachings at the same time. This ability of meditative multitasking was introduced in the previouse chapter and is even more important during this chapter. The next phase to understanding **the Middle Way** is to know the selflessness of things, through their **interdependency** life is connected *on this side of the cardboard sheet as well!*

The following relates to the **theory side of the Middle Way**: All forms share a common beginning, birth, and a common end, decay and corruption. All form *comes about* through *corroboration* with other aspects of phenomena such as earth, air, water, DNA, sexual intercourse, shade, sun-interconnectedness. All things share a common corroboration in that they feed on each other, social interaction, learning, think of an ant colony, millions of individuals working towards one common goal- *working as one highly organized entity!* This is the nature of **Dependant Origination** which states that all things are prone to cause and effect. The meaning- all things are impermanent is not all doom and gloom, it means - all phenomena is in a constant state of change. Your relationship with your attachment included! Further more, no-thing exists inherently except the playing field itself, our dimension for example, it requires no fuel, sunlight or oxygen. That is for everything which exists within it. Trees require water, sunlight, earth while our dimension is its own proof of the eternal, gravity, speed of light, time, these are all constant, permanent, governing factors, the props of this dimension if you will or the conditions. The fact that our form is constantly turning to dust and being remodeled into a dinosaur or a cat also goes to show that the universe waists no-thing. Even our own form is re-used time and again, as is the nature of all conditioned phenomena.

That which arizes dependantly and is thus devoid of inherent existance can be explained as emptiness, the very meaning of emptiness is Dependant Origination.

While the Middle Way is often described as finding a balance between two opposite polarities. This view point is merely the surface or practical representation of the Middle Way. To practice the Middle Way is to;

BE-without attachment, to understand your own EMPTINESS.

And this leads to you <u>no longer projecting your will upon reality!</u>

Dependent Origination : *The existence of objects and phenomena as the result of causes. When one of these causes changes or vanishes, the resulting object or phenomena will also change or disappear, as will the objects or phenomena depending on the changing object itself. Thus, there is nothing (conditioned phenomena) with an eternal self, only mutually dependent origination and existence.*

    This is to acknowledge polarities, to <u>comprehend the nature of this equation</u> *and to not be involved.* When you do not cling or grasp at concepts or idea's, and do not push them away, simply recognize, acknowledge and have no opinion about them, you will find a space. When you find this space, it is like a little surprise, something long forgotten. It makes you stop and pay attention and there is a sort of rising in you, *"Oh yeah, I'd almost forgotten that"* kind of feeling. A feeling in which time seems to stand still and junk simply falls away. When you get there, you don't need to know what to do as there is nothing left *to do.* Do-ing stops being relevant. This is the essence of meditation and for that matter any spiritual peace. Anything you have been doing in the name of spirituality or meditation prior to standing before this doorway is simply wrestling with duality. This space represents the denial of ego and identity and is a good indicator that you are on the right path. Once cultivated in meditation try implementing it in life. You can practice doing this during conversations or during daily activities. The more comfortable you get experimenting with it in daily life as a tool, the easier it will become to implement when the time comes that you will need it as a weapon.

While the practical or surface representation of the Middle Way allows for a calm posture and an easily accessible entrance point for this space during the events of the day, **Lojong** helps you call yourself back from diversions and distractions from your posture. Ultimate truth or reality is *beyond* love and hate, likes and dislikes, it maintains a posture of being neither one, or the other, and so both polarities may *be*. These opposites exist within this singular space. If you like, ultimate truth is impartial to them and even uses them as a form of expression. Hints of this you can witness in the responses of conscious persons as opposed to the totally ignorant. In fact the further you go with this program the stranger the world of modern humans will become. Many things which you previously would brush under the rug become painfully obviouse as anomalies within the balance of harmony. The cause and effect of Karma, positive as well as negative.

If you have even just a lay persons understanding of modern physics you will notice the similarities between what we are talking about here and the nature of the building blocks of everything within our dimension. Buddhism recognizes physics openly. Tiny particles which make up form are constantly popping in and out of our reality *(form/ formless)*, being in two places at the same time and none *(omniscience and emptiness)*, can behave as energy and mass at the same time *(potential to appear as one or the other depending on an "observer". This offers all sorts of potential regarding the power of thought and design in your own destiny)*.

The similarities between the concept of empty space or the field of existence as seen through physics and Buddhism are astounding. These potentials, waves, particles, just as with polarities within ultimate truth, are an expression of the potential of the formless world and part of the world of form at the same time. They exist within it but are oposites. They also have no self expression until consciousness is directed towards them! Ultimate reality is the space, or emptiness, or selflessness which encompass dualistic events allowing these opposing perspectives to co-exist. So yes and no can exist in the same space and due to their impermanent nature they will come and go or one will outweigh the other or even temporarily destroy the other, but the potential for them will endure indefinitely and as one reality. Ultimate reality paradoxically expresses itself through these opposites. In this enormity, the Middle Way offers you the knowledge, understanding and wisdom to master the harmony of living. This is the path way of taking the notion of *not* deflecting dislikes or clinging to likes, then taking it as far as you can possibly run with it.

Theoretical physicist David Bohm painted the picture well when he was explaining his understanding of the nature of the building blocks of our universe, he said this;

It is as meaningless to view the universe as composed of "parts" as it is to view the different geysers in a fountain as separate from the water out of which they flow. Dividing reality up into parts and then naming those parts is always arbitrary, a product of convention, because sub-atomic particles, and everything else in the universe, are no more separate from one another than different patterns in an ornate carpet.

He also said;

Our current way of fragmenting the world into parts not only doesn't work, but may even lead to our own extinction.

This last statement although broad could be reduced to our own situation regarding conceptualizing attachments! While on the subject of similarities from the world of physics, we may also reflect upon the Dalai Lama's words. With the following paragragh he describes the perspective of modern physics with regard to the ___lack of inherent existence___ within phenomena. The perspective of Dependant Origination is perhaps the only concept in the human archijve outside of witch craft which suports the weird and whackey world of quantum physics when it tries to explain reality.

"In classical physics it was assumed that objects posses some kind of self-defining or objective reality. There is a growing understanding that the very notion of reality incorporates the idea of some kind of perspective, and thus there is some inevitable role for consciousness. I have noticed that in quatum physics there are difficulties articulating what reality is. This is because scientists have come to realize that they cannot ground reality in the ___objective status of things.___ *"*

~HH-the Dalai Lama- From Here to Enlightenment~

*

So our inventory for contemplation of **the Middle Way** in preparation for meditation involves the marriage of:

• Deep meditation with; ___special insight and discriminative awareness___ as we have discussed in previous chapters. This is to understand what is meant by the Buddhist concept of *emptiness* which relates to *ultimate truth.*

• Add ___dependent origination___ as we have just discussed, cause and effect shared by all conditioned phenomena. This removes grasping at the self. This relates more to *Samsaric or conventional truth.*

Hold onto this mind set while **avoiding swings of extremes** (over excitement and boredom) between meditation. These are the ingredients for stepping into the practice of the Middle Way.

The same life looking through different eyes, how dare we attach or assume an identity, our directive is to assist all life, not to have an opinion about it.
Life becomes suddenly simple.

*

Understanding our interconnectedness on this side of the cardboard sheet is crucial to defining the essence of the Middle Way, not only is all life "joined at the hip", everything depends on everything else for its existence, cause and effect! On one side of the sheet of card board we have the light ubiquitous symbolizing the oneness of all life in the formless arena, while on the other, we now have dependent arising in which we see another form of inter-reliance and thus unity once again but this time on the form side of the sheet. This could be described simply as a more loosely packed version of the formless side, making the sheet of cardboard (our dimension) merely a sort of temporary, even imagined room divider. Deal with your karma/ negative emotions and you will change your future, the way you effect other entities and your own reality. You will literaly become another person. Cause, effect, change one, change history. The only difference being that on this side of the sheet our interdependence relies on choice and perspective, hence the dualistic nature of our dimension. We can either see our selves as a beam of light which when observed as made up of particles shoots straight out into the darkness until it falters, or as light consisting of waves which create an interference pattern intermingling to serve each others needs.

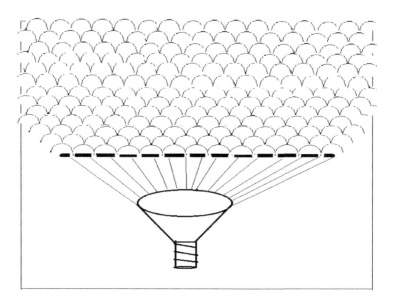

The later is the reality but modern man chooses to look to the earlier description which creates a perspective of isolation, territorial-ism and self gratification, this is what we call commonsensical reality. Weirdly enough physics also states that on the sub-atomic level, particles and wave forms are the same thing, it is a question of *perspective* and both co-exist and do not simultaneously. This again sounds suspiciously like the dualistic aspect of reality encompassed by the field of ultimate truth in which they may both *be*... It is a little like a huge game of dominoes in which what affects the first eventually effects the last playing piece, or a bowl of soup which while the texture varies in density, it remains just a bowl of soup.

Two things strike me as paramount at this point, the absoluteness of interdependency (insinuating the non-identity of all conditioned phenomena) and the fragility of our total existence. Where are we without compassion in such a predicament? If you loath your neighbor but rely on him to *be* your neighbor, not only are you doing yourself a dis-service but when this penny drops we come to realize that such activity is a complete waste of time. Imagine being at war with your neighbor your whole life and this being the main cause of stress in your life. Now imagine realizing the futility of this on your death bed! Suddenly our own disregard for the delicate balance of our existence becomes alarmingly obvious as we start to wake up from the self-gratification stupor. For example the human tendency to put financial progress above nature and the environment or our own tendency to inundate our perfect bodies with poisons in the name of "having a good time"? Or "stress crutch"! These are not part of the program! These are all just little insanities of I-dentity in a Samsaric world of duality and choice. Unfortunately these insanities have very dire consequences.

The Middle Way explains a quantum reality which unfolds in the present moment, like a Hollywood blockbuster constantly unfolding in real time. The choices we make effect the script writing of the film. Our choices when grounded in ultimate truth create a harmonious reality and when we act out of self gratification or wrong view we end up with the holocaust, cause and effect in a quantum evolution. Cancer is also a player in dependent origination which means if we do not turn our attachments around we make ourselves irreversibly sick. Wrong views will also achieve the same result. This sickness is not uncommon and perhaps it is because our leaders do not act upon the planetary side effect of our self gratifying nature that we individualy maintain a jaded stale outlook- we are doing it collectively to the planet, why should it be considered strange to destroy ourselves?

Because once you have looked behind the curtain, you can not turn back! Such a wrong view is a misconception held by an false identity.

*

An explanation of The Middle Way was delivered in the Dhammacakkappavattana Sutta. This was the first teaching of the Buddha upon his awakening. Buddha describes The Middle Way as the path of moderation, a balance between extremes of sensual indulgence and self-mortification.

*Monks, these two extremes ought not to be practiced by one who has gone forth from the household life. (What are the two?) There is **addiction to indulgence** of sense-pleasures, which is low, coarse, the way of ordinary people, unworthy, and unprofitable; and there is **addiction to *self-mortification**, which is painful, unworthy, and unprofitable.*

***Avoiding both these extremes**, the Tathagata (the Perfect One) has realized the Middle Path; it gives vision, gives knowledge, and leads to calm, to insight, to enlightenment and to Nirvana. And what is that Middle Path realized by the Tathagata...? **It is the Noble Eightfold path**, and nothing else, namely: right view, right intention, right speech, right action, right livelihood, right effort, right mindfulness and right concentration.*

*

*(self-mortification refers to ascetic practices in which monks would deprive themselves of almost all nourishment and pleasures)

As such, the Middle Way refers to the the Noble Eightfold Path or Wheel of Dharma as the noble path to achieve Nirvana, instead of taking extremes of austerities and sensual indulgence. To simply read the content of the Wheel of Dharma is not enough, in fact as such it seems a let down or disappointment. The information discussed up till now is required for it to have any impact. Think of the Eightfold Path as a bottle of champagne, the *content*, when shaken up, makes for the ritualistic popping of the cork transforming it into a projectile, just as pimping up our *knowledge* (the antidote for ignorance) creates our understanding leading eventually to enlightenment and release from attachments. The content of the Eightfold Path must also be scrutinized through our new perspective and taken up as code.

You are probably coming to the conclusion that a part of you is at risk of disappearing or dying at this stage. You would be correct in your assumptions. It doesn't happen over night. The automatic response to stimulus in a fight or flight situation always reawakens an aspect of the I-dentity or ego in a human. The mind is a tool and as such it carries out its directive and that is a good thing. Because we are so under the influence of the five senses, we are prone to relapses in our posture and this is why we are vulnerable to attachments and their lure. Sensory perceptions are like Newtonian physics, they're great for the really big stuff but can offer us very little insight or reliable knowledge of the ultimate nature of things. Know this though; with all that you have learned up till now, if you implement it daily, not only will you be released from your attachments but the relapses of I-dentity will also fade. This self, combined with our physical form, is what dies at death. To allow your I-dentity to die through teachings, understanding, and eventually wisdom, is to die a little before you die. While this may be a little disconcerting, you will not be losing anything that you will miss. Things you hold or held dear as aspects of your personality or I-dentity will no longer hold the same attraction nor mean the same thing to you. New things will take their place, this is simply evolution and yours has just become accelerated.

The Heart Sutra

Avalokiteshvara, the Bodhisattva of Compassion, meditating deeply on Perfection of Wisdom, saw clearly that the five aspects (senses) of human existence are empty, and so released himself from suffering.

Answering the monk Sariputra, he said this:

> *Body is nothing more than emptiness,*
> *emptiness is nothing more than body.*
> *The body is exactly empty,*
> *and emptiness is exactly body.*
>
> *The other four aspects of human*
> *existence --*
> *feeling, thought, will, and consciousness*
> *are likewise nothing more than*
> *emptiness,*
> *and emptiness nothing more than they.*
>
> *All things are empty:*
> *Nothing is born, nothing dies,*
> *nothing is pure, nothing is stained,*
> *nothing increases and nothing*
> *decreases.*
>
> *So, in emptiness, there is no body,*
> *no feeling, no thought,*
> *no will, no consciousness.*
> *There are no eyes, no ears,*
> *no nose, no tongue,*
> *no body, no mind.*
> *There is no seeing, no hearing,*
> *no smelling, no tasting,*
> *no touching, no imagining.*
> *There is nothing seen, nor heard,*
> *nor smelled, nor tasted,*
> *nor touched, nor imagined.*

There is no ignorance,
and no end to ignorance.
There is no old age and death,
and no end to old age and death.
There is no suffering, no cause of
suffering,
no end to suffering, no path to follow.
There is no attainment of wisdom,
and no wisdom to attain.

The Bodhisattva's rely on the Perfection
of Wisdom,
and so with no delusions,
they feel no fear,
and have Nirvana here and now.

All the Buddhas,
past, present, and future,
rely on the Perfection of Wisdom,
and live in full enlightenment.

The Perfection of Wisdom is the greatest
mantra
It is the clearest mantra,
the highest mantra,
the mantra that removes all suffering.

This is truth that cannot be doubted.
Say it so:

> *Gaté,*
> *gaté,*
> *paragaté,*
> *parasamgaté.*

Bodhi!
Svaha!

Which means...

Gone,
  gone,
  gone over,
  gone fully over.
  Awakened!
  So be it!

*

Comprehending the Middle Way

Open doorway number 7....

You see a night sky devoid of moon but with extremely bright stars, like pin holes in a dark cloth. To your left and right are two looming mountains adorned with heavy snow fall silver in the starlight. One mountain collects snow blown in by the westerlies and the other is blown in from the east. The western wind delivers poisonous snow, full of smog and pollution created by industry and over population. It is a fell wind and the deposits it leaves behind kill most everything that tries to grow there. The other mountain seems blessed carrying pure snow and clean air which has traveled over the cleanest seas and untouched rain forests. Everything on this mountain is lush and thriving. You step out onto the pathway which meanders through the valley traveling ever downwards between the two mountains.

Immediately you become aware that the snow is in danger of avalanching from both sides. Using your power over form which you have developed through meditation you can keep them from collapsing in and avalanching down upon you. You realize that without your recognition of the danger that you would be leaving everything up to chance, that it is only the power of your acknowledgment which holds the rank, and filthy snow on your left and the pure snow on your right from potentially suffocating you. It takes almost no effort to avoid this potential catastrophe and to hold your middle path between these two radical polarities as you you walk on in confidence and calm towards your goal,~ what's at the end of the path...

You see a light and walk towards it. The valley comes to an end.

There is a wall and in its center a doorway with a small light above it. Turning the door knob you open the door and are smitten with an intense light that seems to be everywhere. Here is the light ubiquitous. You are standing in what appears to be the projector room of a great cinema. Even when you close your eyes you still see the light. As your eyes become accustomed to the light, you start to take an inventory of what is in the room. Not much, two great pipes, one far left, the other far right. Each pipe allows air into the room and the air is carried from the two mountains outside. The bright light is coming form a huge bulb in the center of the room, and as the particles gathered in the air float down to mingle and dance in front of the light bulb, they form a projection on the wall. In front of the light built into the wall where the projection falls is a black sheet punctured with many holes of varying size.

What is on the other side?

You notice another doorway and step through. On this side you enter the viewing room of the cinema lined with empty chairs all facing a huge screen. The pinhole projection created by the particles of dark and light snow and residue drifting in from the mountains is amplified and projected on the screen. At first nothing seems to be happening and you take a seat to continue your observation. As you do so you become aware that you are a witness to this situation and probably not supposed to be here. You are being given an opportunity to observe something quite secret.

The lights reflected on the screen start to move! What you assumed to be inanimate particles of light seem to be alive. Left on their own, these particles of light have started to investigate there environment. They are using what they have to create life on the screen! The projection on the screen is made up of particles gathered from both mountains outside this cinema. The light is life force and the particles are the building blocks which are available to create the image on the screen. The image on the screen becomes a conduit for the particles, here lies the choice, what to build?

The screen has large ugly spots and areas of pristine white. As the areas of white light engulf the screen, its brilliantness spreads through the entire cinema while the ugly spots retreat. The individual conduits on the screen have started to share their knowledge and understanding that in gathering positive pure particles to themselves that their existence becomes more harmonious and peaceful. As the news of this wholesome cause and effect spreads the entire cinema gathers light until it is almost as bright as the light in the projector room. You realize that because the conduit images on the screen no-longer randomly take any old air from the projector room but are specifically attracting air flowing in from the pure mountain that there is simply no market for air from the polluted, foul mountain on the western side!

As the conduit images on the screen choose and more particles adhere to the obvious wisdom of sharing the news of the road to success, the purity of the air and light through out the whole cinema is purged and cleansed. The foul mountain is till there, only in our cinema, our local environment, our personal world has become purged and we can see the truth of existence and the reason for sharing and being compassionate and loving towards those we care about <u>and those we don't!</u>

Looking back over your shoulder, you see the projector sheet with all the pin holes and the intense light shining through. It looks identical to the night sky full of bright stars which you were struck by when you first opened the doorway to room 7 and the now almost white screen with slight shades of dark looks remarkably like the snow covered mountain landscape outside. You realize also that the particles reflected on the screen have no life of their *own and that you are the only "living thing" in the cinema. <u>Your</u> environment is responding to the state of <u>your</u> mind or rather, you have become an integral part of your environment! The realization falls that the barriers and doorways of this world are illusions held in place by wrong views and that when we all can see the true nature of this then we have affected a paradigm shift...*

which heralds the end of Samsara.

*

The wisdom of Dependant Arizing by default offers the wisdom of ultimate truth, hence proper understanding of the true nature of reality-Emptiness.

It, life, consciousness, whatever you want to call it needs to learn and grow, experience things, this is the purpose of existence. There are thousands of worlds and dimensions, ours is Samsaric in nature. We are life, our ticket is our karma, how we deal with our karma affects the show. We are both the actors and the audience. Buddhism states that ignorance is our greatest defect, (they know not what they do...) Buddhism offers us the chance to observe all this from a distance. With this knowledge, we can adjust the way we deal with karma and the byproducts of the karma of others. We can to a certain degree direct reality to help create a more wholesome version of it.

Chapter 8

The Wheel of Dharma

The Buddha's teachings, which are known as "Dharma", are likened to a wheel that moves from country to country in accordance with changing conditions and people's karmic inclinations.

Some of these you have already come across during the reading of this book. I use the Eightfold Path as an essential part of daily meditation having memorized the *essence of each step*. Without full understanding of all of the elements mentioned in this book, the Eightfold Path is merely a set of nice idea's by which to live but with the full understanding offered by the teachings, they become subtle and deep wisdoms. This is why reflection on their roots is required, not just repetition of the verses. Right View (step 1) for example mentions impermanence and karmic conditioning which obviously offers a huge scope to reflect upon, while step 5 simply states that the right sort of employment is important. Without implementing the essence this appears to be simple even shallow. Step 5 is directly bound to giving and your input into the world, to compassion, motivation and perspective. It is also something which many of us see as the most time consuming activity with which we are busy in our daily lives and so if it were to be at loggerheads with our understanding of reality that would be counterproductive to our being, especially if it were something dreadful like selling poison to people who are attached for example. So here we are presented with two aspects of what on the surface appears to be a simple message regarding the nature of our employment which help us observe step 5 in a different light. The doing of without reflection, mechine like, and the other; reflecting upon the reason for the doing of. If you like pre and post awareness. Say you are a bar tender. In the practical scenario one is identifying subconsciously with the lie that it's o.k to sell alcohol to alcoholics, and why not? Society condones the drug, the user and the job, (the pusher, you).

"hey a fella's got to make a living"

or

"If I didn't do this job the next guy will!"

In a world of separation this is normal, that's how we maintain personel for things like war and drilling for oil but in a world of compassion, this involves putting in the hours to build bridges of compromise in your mind, condoning the little white lie through your actions. You, who knows better now, are signing up to societies blind spots. This goes less insidiously against the grain of your teachings making you, the student, a liar. It also nullifies the strength of the things you have learned, making this book merely;

something you have reflected upon and understood but now it's time to get back to the "real world", the world of attachment, abuse and poison.

Seen as such the 8 steps of the path are a guideline for the content or *essence* of the teachings and should be meditated and acted upon as such. A good example of utilizing the essence of the teachings which support the steps would be the explanation of step 7 right mindfulness in chapter 4. When observed superficially, it simply suggests focus on the body, the mind, events and emotions, but seen through the vision of the teachings, a new perspective is offered. Our objective is to identify with these things instead of the destructive reflex behaviors of substance abuse or wrong view.

Step 7, as seen from the perspective of the teachings, brings me straight to the core of calm abiding and restores my sense of self-knowledge and purpose. If I am wrestles and can not find my *chi-spot* even after the candle meditation, I implement step 7 and dwell there before moving on but usually the entire 8 steps in sequence are utilized. Why step 7? Because it centers the individual in his or her I-dentity through reflection upon the form, then the formless aspect of the self. Then it moves on to the recognition of false I-dentity through the nature of phenomena and emotions. It reminds me who and what I am, and brings me in balance with the universe.

Of course the goal of a Bodhisattva is to help others find their way and reduce suffering, but you are in quite a different situation. You are borrowing elements from Buddhism because enlightenment and release from attachments travel the same road. In such a situation try to model it so that you take elements which speak to you regarding the cessation of attachments. Just as the ferry man brings himself to the other side of the river in the second step of the awakening mind of bodhichitta, Imagine yourself and the millions of others suffering attachments at this point in time. Imagine you are taking the helm and ferrying these wretches to the other side. Eventually, when you no longer have any opinion about your attachment, you have become the Shepherd.

The Eightfold Path.

1. Right View

*This is simply the start and finish of the path, it means to see things as they are as one complete. As such, right view is the cognitive aspect of wisdom. **It means to see through things, to grasp the impermanent and imperfect nature of worldly objects and ideas, and to understand the law of karma and karmic conditioning.** Right view has very little to do with any intellectual capacity, just as wisdom is not just a matter of intelligence. Instead, right view is attained, sustained, and enhanced through all capacities of mind during meditation. It begins with the intuitive insight that all beings are subject to suffering and it ends with complete understanding of the true nature of all things.*

- *This is directly refering to special insight.*

*

2. Right Intention

*Right view refers to the mechanical aspect of wisdom and, right intention addresses the forward push of our understanding. This is all about **commitment to ethical and mental self-improvement**. Buddha describes three types of right intention:*

1. *Denial of desire.*

2. *Renunciation of volatile negative emotion.*

3. *The intention of harmlessness,_ : do not think or act out of aggression, develop compassion. Approach this concept of harmlessness from the corner of the bodhichitta.*

- *This encompasses renunciation of the ego and knowledge of the nature of desire. Be mindful of your reaction to the 3rd step.*

*

3. Right speech

*Right speech embraces ethical conduct in the eightfold path. Ethical conduct is an expression of **moral discipline**, which is the foundation of all the other principles of the path. This aspect is essential and takes work and cultivation. Words can destroy or save lives, make enemies or friends, start or create war and peace:*

1.   to <u>abstain from false speech</u>

2.   to <u>abstain from slanderous speech</u>

3.   to <u>abstain from harsh words</u>

4.   to <u>abstain from idle chatter</u>

• *Listen to yourself.*

*

4. Right Action

Right action is the follow up of right intention. It is your physical expression which is an act of creation within the field. This is to take full responsibility for the outward expression of your thought. Within the parameters we have been given, our actions are an expression of our attention to karma. Unwholesome actions lead to unsound states of mind, while **wholesome actions lead to sound states of mind***. Right action means*

1.   *to abstain from harming sentient beings, to abstain from taking life (including suicide)*

2.   *to abstain from taking what is not given,*

3.   *to abstain from sexual misconduct.*

*

5. Right Livelihood

To earn a living in a wholesome manner. Ones efforts should never harm others, the environment or our ethics. The Buddha describes this as not selling weapons, drugs, being in the military or working in slaughter houses, being involved in prostitution or slavery.

Also avoid anything involving sweat shops or slave/ child labor and if possible support local cottage industry as opposed to corporations.

*

6. Right Effort

Involves dealing with energy prior to, or in the act of carrying it out. Your effort can express itself in either wholesome or unwholesome states. **The same energy that fuels desire, envy, aggression, and violence can fuel self-discipline, honesty, benevolence, and kindness.**

(The one you feed)

Be mindful of the following

1. <u>Prevent the arising of un arisen unwholesome states,</u>

2. <u>Abandon unwholesome states that have already arisen,</u>

3. <u>Arouse wholesome states that have not yet arisen, and</u>

4. <u>Maintain and perfect wholesome states already arisen.</u>

• *Correct diligence and concentration. Being on guard regarding distractions of the ego, make your effort count. Remember the Gollum sitting on your shoulders with his fingers around your neck? This is him either tightening his grip or writhing in his death throes.*

*

7. Right Mindfulness

*Right mindfulness is the controlled and **perfected faculty of cognition.** It is the mental ability to see things as they are, with clear consciousness. The normal thought process is based on judgment, attachment or clinging to old concepts from the past and then an image or concept is formed around an object, person or event. 90% of our perception is formed by these impressions, 10% is actual reality. This happens in the subconscious. Right mindfulness is anchored in clear perception and it penetrates impressions without getting carried away. Right mindfulness allows us to grip the process of conceptualization in a way that actively observes and controls the direction of our thoughts. Buddha explains this with four foundations of mindfulness:*

1. *Contemplation of the <u>body</u>,*

2. *Contemplation of the <u>state of mind</u>,*

3. *Contemplation of the <u>phenomena</u>, and*

4. *Contemplation of <u>feeling</u> (repulsive, attractive, or neutral)*

- *This refers to Dependant Origination*

*

8. Right Concentration

This involves training the mind to focus correctly, with every -single- aspect, and to maintain this but without effort. This can only be achieved through regular meditation. Rigpa allows us to direct our thought process and control our mind. Right concentration involves one pointedness of mind embracing all aspects of cognition towards wholesome expression. Right concentration is the act of incorporating all 7 of these first steps and building this process into daily life.

*The eighth principle of the path, right concentration, refers to the development of a mental force that occurs in natural consciousness, although at a relatively low level of intensity, namely concentration. Concentration in this context is described as **one-pointedness of mind**, meaning a state where all mental faculties are unified and directed onto one particular object. Right concentration for the purpose of the eightfold path means wholesome concentration, i.e. concentration on wholesome thoughts and actions. The meditating mind focuses on a selected object or situation. It first directs itself onto it, then sustains concentration, and finally intensifies concentration step by step all the while being mindful of perspective. Through practice it becomes natural to apply elevated levels concentration also in everyday situations.*

*

Perfect mind and body

I abused myself with soft drugs and alcohol from the time I was thirteen. Before that I couldn't wait to get started with it all because that is what I had seen around me since 0. Not to mention it was already in my DNA before I was born and in my anscetsory. Around sixteen, I also started experimenting with pills and powders eventually moving on to cocaine and LSD. Some of the kids I work with today are thirteen (my age when I first started dabbling) and I cannot for the life of me imagine them partying hard and doing what I did. Granted I was an "old youth" in that I had experienced much and traveled a lot as a kid attending a total of fourteen different schools. I was also making some money as a musician at an early age and left home around my sixteenth birthday. These things combined with a lack of parental guidance and some very bad influences made me the I-dentity I was for better or worse. I must also add that the constant bombardment of drugs and alcohol subdued my mind which didn't want to be confronted with events of my youth. They actually served a purpose but due to their nature they always deliver the suffering of change.

Before the drugs and alcohol I was a runner. I had grown up running with my dog through the bush, with my mother or alone. It looked like I might have even had a future in it. I used to be the star runner in my age group at the Brisbane Boys Grammar school before it became impossible to continue.

This is not an ego rant, I am suggesting that as humans we have the power to go in whatever direction we choose at all times. When all aspects of us are 100% focused in the same direction and the mind is convinced of its goal, the human machine is an entity to be reckoned with. It has the power to move providence. It can, with equal zeal and fervor, destroy itself. Remember the wolves, the one you feed? Those temporary moments of so-called release from so-called suffering which you experience while using are determining moments. Brick by brick you are building the story of your life and feeding one wolf or the other. You can always stop and when you do you can revert to the athletic 13 year old at almost any time in your life. I am not kidding. I will be 50 next birthday and I look fitter and feel better than I can *ever* remember. Not to get ahead of ourselves though, the laying of those bricks takes up much time, and your time on this plane is limited, which means the story your life has an end. The sooner you revert to a natural state of mind and body the sooner you can start building the remainder of your story as a joyful, positive and peacefuller, loving existence.

Your physical performance will improve in every aspect and this reflects strongly on your psychological posture. You will start to act out of a desire to reach different goals. Indeed *you* are no longer! The new perspective allows you to discover who you really are and what you really want instead of living a deluded life surrounding yourself with all of the shit orbiting around your attachment.

One of the last strongholds of my attachments was an old ship which I had purchased when I was still well off, prior to the collapse of my business. Due to my bankruptcy I couldn't afford to maintain it any more but it still represented all the romantic trappings of an old ship while I would sit there drinking, watching it fall apart. Those refreshing little weekends onboard would usually require another weekend just to recover.When I quit my attachments it quickly changed from one reality to another. To my horror, I had become a sheddy, a guy with a man cave! Where previously it was a place I could escape to, alone or with drinker friends, where I could drop anchor and drink whilst flying the flag of "a sailing weekend", it had now become a rotting nightmare. As a sober person I quickly realized that it would take me every waking moment to fix it up on my own, and due to the collapse of my business, I was alone! I could hardly afford my attachment let alone a 20 meter wooden sail boat riddled with rot!

In those patches of quitting using the will power method I wouldn't even visit the boat. After 12 years, I realized I was not a sailor and had better things to do with my time than dishing out a fortune on repairs only so I could dish out a fortune on self destruction. Owning a sail boat has one thing in common with drug abuse, they are both akin to a hole in the ocean that you try to fill up with money! Twelve years and many tens of thousands of euro's later I realized how much time, money and energy I had just burned through. The only consolation I have is that there are actually some fantastic memories of events I would have otherwise not experienced had I followed a different road. Strangely though these memories are not memories of using or of my attachment but rather memories of moments of sobriety and flashes of fantastic expressions of nature experienced on board. The rest is really a bit of a blur.

You may have a negative self-image or an idea that you are fat, stupid, bad genes, a loser, what ever. If you have read this book to this point then you are not stupid, or a loser and obesity or unwanted fat usually has a lot to do with your attachment. Bad genes or a physical defect is not an excuse, any ailment you have will become drastically minimized as soon as you quit. Problems that appear to be ji-normouse are easy to solve when you are well and not absorbing depressants or stimulants. I am not suggesting you will only have good days, I am telling you that whatever happens you will be better equipped to deal with *anything*. Including:

the absurd nonsense of detox!

Trust me on this, I am an expert. I have quit and gone through the most dreadful detox pains, sweats, throwing up the works. I have also quit the same substance using a different method and had almost no problem with it. The trigger mechanisms for detox pains and withdrawal nonsense are caused or disarmed by *your perspective* of three points.

- The difference comes when you give up because you have seen through the trick, you know what your attachment is and understand who and what you are.

When you **KNOW THIS;**

> *You quit because you want to, not because you think you must and are depriving yourself of something of value. You understand you are missing out on **NOTHING**.*

- The little Gollum whispering in your ear telling you that you body needs to top up its poison level. This is the same for a coffee drinker or someone who drinks energy drinks or eats chocolate in front of the T.V. every night. It feels like hunger and that's not so bad!

- The MAD strip figure who doesn't say much but is always reminding you of habitual behavior, such as when you feel any stimulus from the world you grab for a cigarette or when you reflect on some horror from your child hood you reach for the bottle, even just the reflex of doing something with your hands, whatever, this is akin to having an itch and resisting the temptation to scratch it. It soon dies.

This adds up to you being mildly frustrated at times and experiencing something physically which is akin to have a cold. It lasts for about 4 days and after a week is completely gone for good. I don't know anybody who *really knows* they are addicted who wouldn't trade it in for a bout of the flu only to be done with it for ever after a week! If you analise the detox pains with an open mind or from an objective point of view, they are a little like hunger as suggested. Although some other methods may tell you to substitute the object of your attachments with nothing I differ. If you can ease the "pain" temporarilly do it! Distract yourself with it if you want. This will help:

SUGAR

Especially if it's alcohol you are giving up. This sort of replacement should be reduced after a few weeks or replaced with some other harmless T.V. snack without sugar such as nuts or dried fruit. Whether you are quitting a substance with sugar in it or not, candy or sugary snax will greatly reduce any withdrawal symptoms. Marijuanha, coke, cigarettes, alcohol and heroin all effect the blood sugar levels.

Another thing people winge and moan about when they quit is;

It's dreadful, I couldn't sleep at all!

This is a strange one. People with attachments usually have grown accustomed to calling sleep that thing that they do when they pass out drunk or stoned for at least a 10 hour recovery snooze. This is not sleep, it is closer to coma than sleep and sure, you're usually in it before you hit the pillow. When you get used to your new way of being, you will sleep like a baby and wake up like an athlete full of energy and ready for another great day. So what if you can't sleep for a couple of nights, it happens. It only becomes a big deal if you think you are making a sacrifice and you know this to be untrue. Remember it is part of the cure and that makes it a positive thing.

Those dreadful withdrawal pains and yes even the physiological symptoms are largely aspects of your I-dentity faking it, terrified of losing anything with which it identifies. Why?

Because this signifies the onset of cognitive dissonance and potentially threatens its own existence.

Any suffering you do experience is a measure of your development on the road to your enlightenment and or release and as such is a gaining of merit.

Remember the detox symptoms are a reminder that you have quit and every time you feel them, visualize your self beating the shit out of that demon on your back. Feel his grip loosen with each failing onslaught.

*Your suffering is the suffering of your demons dying!

In fact it may be time for you to start slaying hungry ghosts during meditation!

Demons demise

Upon entering room 6 you become aware of the lack of colour, everything is grey, damp and moldy and there is a stench of death and decay in the air. Take time to imprint this room in all its neglect. The cracked rooftile is gone, now there is a gaping hole through which water streams freely down onto the floor. The carpets are damp and suck at your toes and the flat of your feet. There is a violent storm outside. You are the witness of this situation but at the same time you see yourself on the bed lying wretched and sick. The windows are open and the wind, leaves and rain blow through the room. Next to the bed are your two friends Gollum and MAD figure. You are not conscious and they are trying to rip the soul out of your body, screaming and laughing with glee.

You know where the base ball bat is, now there are 9 inch nails hammered through the business end of it. Take the bat with both hands, stride forwards and get as much swing room as you can. As you bring the bat down on the pathetic figure of Gollum, feel the impact and hear the puncturing of the nails and splintering of bone. See the blood spatter out across the walls. Take a swing at the MAD figure. This idiotic character vanishes in a puff of smoke, as ineffectual in departure as it ever was in anything, except to remind you to light up. As you beat the Gollum creature into the corner of the room you realize it has lost consciousness. As it now lies bleeding, surrounded by a culdesac of blood spatters. You drop the bat, take up the weight of the unconscious body and push it up the wall onto the window ledge. Outside the window is a clicko, a large garbage can waiting with the lid open. Roll the body over the ledge and watch it slide/ fall down the weather boards into the clicko, ready for the garbage collector.

As the body thumps down into the clicko the rain lessens and the sun begins to break through the clouds. Slowly you notice the colour returning to the room as the light shines through the open window. The other you remains on the bed unconscious but now you can begin to heal. The life is no longer being drained out of you. Soon you will recover and take care of the disarray of your room.

*

There is no specific moment at which you kill your demons, there are many. This visualization is one you practise as you approach the time of quitting and there after. I would prescribe using it for about a week either side of quitting and then when ever (if ever) you feel the need to revert to it.

Understanding Commitment

Until one is committed, there is hesitancy.

The chance to draw back, always ineffectiveness.

Concerning all acts of initiative (and creation),

there is one elementary truth, the ignorance of which

kills countless ideas and splendid plans: That the

moment one definitely commits oneself, then

providence moves too. All sorts of things occur to help

one that would never otherwise have occurred.

A whole stream of events issues from the decision,

raising in ones favor all manner of unforeseen incidents

and meetings and material assistance, which no man

could have dreamed would come his way.

~Anonymous, A Scottish Himalayan mountain climbing expedition~

*

~QUIT~

Chapter 9

Tantra-Imaginative Meditation.

There is no world outside the mind. There is no real world. The world is actually more dreamlike than we think. So we can recreate reality, and we do, every moment, with our thoughts and projections.

You are probably beginning to get nervous sensing that the time to quit is approaching. This is true, it is approaching, and it's normal for you to be nervous but hold onto the fact that the part of you that is getting concerned is that part you want to get rid of. It's only logical that as the time draws near it will struggle for survival. Use these moments to remind yourself of this and instead of dwelling on the "negative" aspects of quitting, focus on the positive. Remember the advice of the survivalist?

"the most important thing to take with you in a survival situation is a positive frame of mind."

This is a survival situation so take the advice. You are about to embark on an adventure, and on the other side of this event, *you will not be the same.* I shouldn't be saying that because it seems as if something big is about to happen, and it is but the thing which is big is not the quitting, it's what comes after. People who use a substance to dull their mind to reality often tend to deny themselves their true purpose in life. This is not necessarily due to the attachment, but part of the game of wrong views. During our lives we often make compromises like when we leave school wanting to become a doctor but due to our grades we have to become a lawyer for example. If we had tried harder or were smarter then perhaps.....

This is a chronic problem which goes further than being smarter or trying harder, this is a statement about the structure of our society and the way we are raised. Because we live in the paradigm of Samsara (our modern human society), our parents and authority figures like school teachers are obliged to push the Samsaric envelope. This is what they understand to be correct. Such a statement will create defense mechanisms in almost any who hear it for the same reasons you get nervous as the moment of your freedom draws near. An I-dentity does not want to face its short comings or part with an element of its portfolio which reinforces it. I don't want to get involved in presenting a case for why this is so, I want to explain to you that you have made compromises along the way and are probably not living the life you thought you would be when you were younger. Dreams often do not come true and we tend to accept our place in society as our lot, as if there is no alternative. This is one of the main reasons for the hum of unease in the background of civilized life. Hence the need for distractions from "reality".

You may not be the person in the paragraph above and you may be in denial but you are reading this and that means some form of dysfunction brought you here. I am simply making the case for 95% of the people on the planet. If you fit into the 5% that have another reason for your attachment, it doesn't matter the mechanisms are the same. The wonderful thing about all this is;

When you quit your attachment you become available to follow your true purpose in life.

You may not even know what it is and that's fine, but through your transformation

you will evolve.

Not knowing how you will change is also fine, it's an adventure, and the unknown is the exciting part of any adventure. If you do have an idea, that's also great, you can start to build an image of the great things you want to achieve when you are full of energy, positive motivation, better equipped financially. Not only will your mind and body completely evolve;

Every single aspect of your life is about to change for the better.

for ever.

Tantric Meditation

The goal of Tantra is to provide a faster path so that qualified practitioners may be of benefit to others more quickly. The method is to utilize imagination to visualize yourself as already enlightened, as a fully fledged Buddha.

Behind doorway number 9!

1. *Witness yourself from a space of rigpa and see your mind as clear, with all troubling negative emotions replaced by a pure omniscient wisdom and compassion for all sentient beings. Bind deeply with emptiness as learned through the Middle Way.*

2. *Out of the emptiness allow your perfect deity body to come forth. Clean and purged of all attachments, strong, fit and healthy.*

3. *Create an environment as peaceful and abundant as you can imagine and allow this to emit from your deity body. A space in which all beings may find rest and piece of mind.*

*

Imaginative meditation can help you manifest the object of your meditation. This does not mean that you can imagine your way to becoming a Buddha, it means you can visualize the qualities, lifestyle and posture to create an image to which you aspire. Visualize a perfect being, yourself as you want to be -free and full of inquisitive energy, zest for life. A self who has gone through the fire and come out the other side at peace with the new knowledge and way of being. Of course the purpose of this for a Buddhist is to help others and although you must first help yourself, you will directly help others, starting with those who care about you. When practicing Tantra, focus on those you love and how much joy you will bring to them with your transformation.

As a guitarist, I used to imagine the piece of music I was trying to learn. At the conservatorium we were expected to be able to recite long pieces of classical music which were quite complex. To memorize them and help perform them to the best of my ability I found imagining that I was playing them a quicker, more effective method of binding with the piece rather than painstakingly repeating them over and over until they became reflex. This means imagining yourself as healed and at peace with the world is creating an imprint, bringing the thought into the world of form. There are many examples of studies that have proven this to be true. Just google Charles Garfield NASA if you want to check it out for your self. He is one of many who have carried out extensive research in this field.

Using Tantra, you can build the image into Lojong which you can recall upon need. You can also attach this image to a small talisman or object which you can carry with you during the day. During moments in which you feel the need to reinforce your resolve or to recall this image, hold the talisman in your pocket and make the connection.

**It is dangerous to practice this without having followed the steps in this book as you will be deluding yourself and dulling the mind with time wasting practices. It will work against your future abstinence. True Tantric meditation requires a master, initiation and vows, this is adapted to fit your purposes.

At the beginning of Tantric meditation, focus first on emptiness and selflessness as understood through the Middle Way. Become as entwined as you can with emptiness and when you are soaked with it, bring your imagined deity form forth out of the emptiness. Now focus on the deity in all his perfection. Imagine the deity rebuilding his environment- room 6 to start with. The deity simply meditates and focuses upon areas in disrepair within room 6. Through the power of your deity's will alone the walls for example become stripped and sanded and repainted in a coat so thick and strong it would appear to be an enamel coating. The carpets must be replaced or torn out (mine has a polished wood floor). The blood stains in the corner will eventually have to be cleaned up but we leave them till last. This corner will act as a reminder until it's time.

When you do come to clean that last corner of the room, really be there. Picture your self cleaning away the blood stains with a bucket of soapy water on your knees. Not as a deity, as you, but save this till last. Feel the waters temperature and texture, the feel of the rag as you squeeze out the blood and water into the bucket. Hear the water fall from the rag to the bucket. These are important visualizations, this is the blood of your soon to be dead enemy.

A very sacred moment is the replacing of the roof tile. Before the rains come you must visualize this, but it is also something you only have to do when you actually quit. When that time comes feel every step, take the ladder out from under the house climb up on the roof tile in hand. All my roof tiles are grey, the one I am using to replace the old broken one is white. Every time I walk in the room from this time forward I can look up and remember when I see the underbelly of the white roof tile.

*

~QUIT~

Chapter 10

The End of Suffering

I remember my drinking days, the first half of the first glass was hassle free then I was already concerned about the rest of the bottle running out. What a ridiculous waste of time,

and everything else in the universe.

If you feel the need to get smashed or smoke or drink your self stupid do it now or plan it in to do it tonight or *very* soon. Do not wait too long to return to the final phase of the book. That means

SET A DATE.

NOW!

It is O.K. To feel nervous even excited, I know I was thrilled, and when the aha moment came.... There is a moment when you know that you are done with it. It may come months after you have quit, it may have already come half way through this book. It will come and the sensation of release is the most euphoric sensation there is.

FREEDOM!

In a week everything about your life will be healing and you will feel

ABSOLUTELY FANTASTIC!

I never did have a last fag when I quit smoking, I was done way before the end of the book. When I quit drinking using Easy Way, I would always have a last binge and hangover and read the last chapter. If you feel the need to do this then by all means do so but what ever it is you are taking, take the time to truly comprehend what it is you are doing, how it feels, what it tastes like. Feel the negative aspects of your

EX-ATTACHMENT

Especially the hangover. I remember focusing on the last time I got drunk. I really tried to focus on what it was that I actually liked about doing it and couldn't find anything physical I could put my finger on. In fact I recall one part of the Easy Way program in which Allen Carr suggest you sit in a room with no distractions and no company and get drunk. The exercise was to pin point the effect without anything else, then all you have is the effect without colouring. Quickly you will realize that it is the events which happen during your using which make the situation enjoyable and that the act of getting drunk itself is actually a downright bore. Try it if you must. The only "reason" to drink is to lower your guard so that you are not shy when interacting but I guess you already know that tends to back fire. If you were to video the situation you would come to realize that the more intoxicated you become, the less inhibitions you have until you are the biggest arse hole at the party.

So, if you must, now is the point at which you decide to quit and read on, or give yourself

ONE LAST BINGE

Do what you must then re-read from <u>chapter 9</u> to the end of the book. If you feel unsure then there is something you have not understood and you should read the book again and follow all meditations, making sure that all steps are understood.

*

I Waited till the end to implement this next segment as now you hold all the cards and can fully understand the psychological make up and breakdown of attachment. There is discrepancy regarding the addictive personality. AA will tell you it exists and Allen Carr will tell you it's poppy cock. I can tell you it is very real and it can be easily explained through data gathered during research into a certain disorder finally proving it one way or the other. So, the bad news is it does exist. The good news is, using this method, you already have the tools to deal with it. This represents no problem for you what so ever. Now you need to know about it to comprehend the difference between the so-called normal people and the so-called addictive personality. Soon you will be bullet proof and at this stage of the game the knowledge will help you as opposed to before, if you had chosen not to finish the book you may have been walking around with half informations which could have hurt you badly.

The science behind it is very straight forward;

It has been proven that the EEG frequency at which the brain of a child between zero and 2 years operates is (predominantly) 0.5 to 4 cycles per second (Hz) with short bursts of higher activity. From 2-6 years the activity reads predominantly 4-8 Hz. This lower frequency allows young children to take huge amounts of information on board which explains why I will never be able to speak Dutch as well as a person who is born in Holland. When a brain operates at a lower frequency it is also in a more suggestive

*state, much like hypnosis, which allows access for
information storage into the vastness of the deep sub
conscious setting the information in stone. It also explains
the child prodigy phenomena. Mozart was put behind a
piano regularly since his birth and no doubt was surrounded
by music even in the womb.*

~Aquarius Agenda -J.M.King~

The **Addictive Personality** could be described as the child
devoid of stability, who learns that he must hold onto and or
destroy anything he identifies with for all he's worth, otherwise it
will be taken from him. This generally ends up with the child and
or later adult pushing things and people away, smashing
relationships, work stability, home environment, problems with
authority figures, society in general, insane jealousy, claiming
behaviour, hysteria by cognative dissonance. What we have
described here is ironically known as **Attachment Disorder**. The
above mentioned pattern is not the only set of symptoms belonging
to this disorder, there are different forms of attachment disorder,
some people become overly passive allowing situations to fly by
without making an effort to grab them. Other people may have
many friends but if you search deeply you will find them to be
superficial friendships or very one sided. The scope of the sickness
makes it hard to pin down however those who are considered to be
addicted to something, anything have a common thread. One in
three adults are carrying attachment disorders and 70% of all so
called addicts have attachment disorders, so I guess we aren't far
off the mark dropping the word addict for attached.

There is enough literature on attachment disorders available
so I won't go into detail here. I would advise *not* seeing a doctor or
taking any pills for this. If you have read this book and have
carried out the exercises, then you already have the tools to deal

with it, I promise. Perhaps you have already stumbled upon this conclusion all by yourself. I did. I knew everything about my condition before I researched attachment disorders. I was at a seminar regarding "basic trust" for my work when the lecturer started talking about attachment disorders and addiction. Suddenly my jaw dropped, I even wrote home to tell my mother what she and her siblings were suffering from! It has a name! Unfortunately my news was not taken on board, infact it was met with a strong bout of denial. Also a very standard reaction.

Flores believes that addicts, even before their addiction kicks in, struggle with knowing how to form emotional bonds to connect to other people.While it's commonly understood that early childhood attachments to parents and family are necessary for healthy development, Flores says, emotional attachments remain necessary throughout adulthood. It's not enough, he says, to "just stop drinking." To achieve long-term well-being, addicts need opportunities to forge healthy emotional attachments.

Flores reports that this is the reason for the phenomenal success rate of Alcoholics Anonymous over more than 50 years. When people walk into an A.A. meeting, the whole point is to admit openly that they are an alcoholic and yet to feel fully accepted for exactly who they are, with no condemnation. What a relief! This experience of, in essence, pure attachment, may be the best attachment experience in their lives – and most people who walk in and experience this, miraculously, stay sober for decades or a lifetime.

~Philip J Flores PhD -Addiction as an Attachment Disorder~

The constant state of fear and or anxiety is a direct result of this disorder. It is accepted, by the one suffering the disorder as *"the way it is"* and why not, he or she has never known any better. This is one of the reasons we search for escapism. Treatment comes through meditation or hypnotherapy not pills and not doctors! The information in this book is absolutely sufficient to deal with this disorder but it takes a little time due to the subconscious and deep seated nature of reflex wrong view implemented during early childhood. Feel free to research this disease, just be careful with any advised treatments, the pharmaceutical companies are always busy with ways to get people to take pills for their entire lives which are designed not to cure but to hook in a life long patient as a source of income. Sound familiar? You would do better to use tantric meditation imagining yourself as a self healing shaman, swapping one drug to cure another is absolute lunacy and an insult to your intelligence.

Here are a few causes of this disorder;

- A baby cries and no one responds or offers comfort.

- A baby is hungry or wet, and they aren't attended to for hours.

- No one looks at, talks to, or smiles at the baby, so the baby feels alone.

- A young child gets attention only by acting out or displaying other extreme behaviors.

- A young child or baby is mistreated or abused.

- Sometimes the child's needs are met and sometimes they

aren't. The child never knows what to expect.

- The infant or young child is hospitalized or separated from his or her parents.

- A baby or young child is moved from one caregiver to another (can be the result of adoption, foster care, or the loss of a parent).

- The parent is emotionally unavailable because of depression, an illness, or a substance abuse problem. The other possibility is that the parent simply doesn't want to be a parent.

As the examples show, sometimes the circumstances that cause the attachment problems could happen now and then, we all have busy lives etc etc. It's not a question of now and then though, complexes come from chronic repeated abuse and neglect while the child is too young to understand what has happened and why. To a young child, it just feels like no one cares and they lose trust in others while the world becomes an ever more unsafe place.

The "insatiable hunger" tends to come from abandonment issues experienced while the child's cognitive abilities are still being formed in combination with observing how our "roll models" deal with their stuff. The "poor kid"in you is merely trying to fill a void or hole in the soul which cannot be filled no matter how much excess you throw at it. Of course one can never fill the hole this way but you can be removed from it for a little while, even black it out if you like. This absorbing of information under stress and during early growth develops subconscious behaviors cementing them so deeply that they could be considered personality traits. This could always go both ways extreme smoker but anti alcohol, or extreme non smoker heavy drinker, there is no half way. Even if you think you know some one who fits the bill but doesn't seem to have an issue, the truth will come out sooner or later and will be expressed as some sort of odd posture towards smoking, drinking, sexuality or wrong view whatever the attachment is. These reflexes are imprinted on the soul and expressed outwardly in social (or should I say anti- social) activities and postures.

Fear not if you think you fit this bill! Buddhism suggests that you chose this path, your karma gave you this path to work on. And you now understand the nature of the addictive personality through understanding the true nature of attachment, I-dentity and reality. Mind control, meditation, can repair the addictive personality issue, as I have said it is a program of anti-brain washing. Nothing else can remove it as effectively as meditation, it is as effective as surgery. Finally, you understand through the wisdom of the Middle Way that choice will offer you your destiny and that providence will hold your hand all the way! You are lucky to be using the only existing permanent, non-will power solution to your problem, if you are this personality profile. I know this to be true as I am one of these profiles and I have danced with this rubbish my entire life. All you have to do is take providence by the hand and run with it! I stopped smoking with Easy way and stopped permanently, though it didn't work with drinking and some wrong view issues. Why? Because I had the attachment to wrong views and alcoholism imprinted in my brain. It was my Achilles heal so to speak. Out of all the shit I took repeatedly, the one that really hooked me in was alcohol and that was because every day from the time I was born until my seventh birthday I would sit across from my grand mother and grand father and watch them get drunk and abuse each other horribly, just us three.

Through the practice of meditation and the study of Dzogchen I have learned to do away with my negative posture and also learned that eventually we must all become our own mothers and fathers. Our greatest addiction is our I-dentity and through this project you will have come to realize that you must first die a little to live completely. This is pertinent now more than ever as your children may need to recover from your parenting even more than you from yours. Much of this has to do with the rapidly increasing awareness and technology of modern humanity. Unfortunately the good and the bad are on the up and up only the bad is often hidden from us or masked as the good. The learning curve was much more gradual for our grandparents and their parents due to a more relaxed streaming of information, the pre-technological revolution. In my life time alone I have witnessed an information explosion which has radically changed my direction and understanding of the world thanks to the internet.

Another very important thing to remember is that you are not making any sacrifice, so don't. In the coming week you shouldn't change a thing. Keep going to work and if you have parties, go to them. Using this method means you are not like one of those poor saps who have stopped using a will-power method. You do not have to avoid situations and most certainly do not have to worry about temptation.

You have quit because you choose to!

This means you are NOT one hit away from being attached at any and every moment. I have to clarify something here. This doesn't mean you can drink/ snort/ smoke/ shoot up and stop when you feel like it, then you will be back to your normal quota in no time. Quitting means you don't do something anymore. I am driven crazy by people who say they have quit then half an hour later I walk outside only to find them sitting in a corner with a smoker, puffing away like a professional on a bummed fag. The response is then;

"I can take it or leave it"

Take notice of these people, they are not what we call non smokers or non drinkers, they are something called a

LIAR!

If you feel *temptation at any point,* this is a warning sign that you are no longer utilizing the power of this method. That is a dangerous thing and the first thing that should come to mind if and when that alarm rings is this:

DOUBT- is the awakening of your I-dentity. Once you have quit your attachments using this method, you do not want to be that I-dentity anymore. This means if you were ever to give in to that drink, shot or snort, you would be opening the doorway for that old I-dentity. This represents a much greater loss than that of sobriety, you will lose your peace of mind and your old baggage will return in its entirety.

*

Keep going to parties and do not change a thing. You may find if you are used to going to the pub to play darts that it's not so interesting anymore but if that is your want then do it. You'll probably either stop after a short while or keep going but only to catch up with old friends and you'll find that you probably won't stay long. If you do this to be sociable there are better places to be sociable anyway. And remember true friends will meet you outside the pub if they are true friends.

I wrote this book because I want the world to be a better place. Armed with this new information you must now also understand that your speedy salvation and indeed evolution also effects me! I was so amazed in the quality of my life when I was finally free and had realized that I had a

PAINLESS & PERMANENT CURE

to my subconscious reactive behaviors. Believe me, I had tried everything 5 times over. When it hit me that I had something in my hands that was unique and had the potential to help such a wide group of people suffering, I had no other option. Substance abuse is the biggest killer on the planet and before it kills the host, it makes the users life and that of his loved ones a misery almost from the first hit till the last. This cure while effective as a cure for attachments is also a window into the philosophy and religion of Buddhism offering insights into human interaction. While it's a great method of self help with attachments, the teachings suggest a higher way or path if you will. It also offers you tools to deal with any or at least many psychological issues which may have plagued you up until now. Deep down I hope this has helped you in more ways than one and that you carry it with you, that it may enrich your life as it has mine.

While the day you quit may not be the happiest day of your life, it will be the day that makes it possible for you to have many, many happy moments in your life which you otherwise would have missed. Welcome to the first day of the rest of your life. It's behind door number 10!

Go for it!

The most wonderful thing about having no attachments is you suddenly wake up to who you are and what you really want to do,

-go do it-

*

Great books which have helped directly or indirectly with this book.

The Fundamental Wisdom of the Middle Way   *Nargarjuna's Mulamadhyamakakarika*

The Tibetan Book of Living and Dying   *Sogyale Rinpoche*

Stages of Meditation   *HH the Dalai Lama*

How to Practise   *HH the Dalai Lama*

Ancient Wisdom Modern World   *HH the Dalai Lama*

the Art of Happiness   *HH the Dalai Lama*

From here to Enlightenment   *HH the Dalai Lama*

The Middle Way   *HH the Dalai Lama*

A Philosophy of Freedom   *Rudolf Steiner*

Knowledge of Higher Worlds   *Rudolf Steiner*

Possible Human Evolution   *P. Ouspenski*

A New Earth   *Eckhart Tole*

The Power of Now   *Eckhart Tole*

Biology of Belief   *Bruce Lipton*

Easy Way to Stop Smoking   *Allen Carr*

Easy Way to Control Alcohol   *Allen Carr*

From Normal to Healthy   *George Kuhlewind*

Addiction as an Attachment Disorder   *Philip J Forbes.*

*

~QUIT~

Printed in Great Britain
by Amazon

23964978R00111